About the Author

I live and work within the great state of Michigan. I picked up writing at a young age. Starting as a diary, soon evolved into poetry; which has branched into many aspects of life. I enjoy the outdoors, traveling, and spending quality time with my family and friends. My dream has been to share my passion of writing with the world.

Naked: Pieces from Beginnings

Derek Hartsel

Naked: Pieces from Beginnings

Olympia Publishers
London

www.olympiapublishers.com
OLYMPIA PAPERBACK EDITION

Copyright © Derek Hartsel 2023

The right of Derek Hartsel to be identified as author of
this work has been asserted in accordance with sections 77 and 78
of the Copyright, Designs and Patents Act 1988.

All Rights Reserved

No reproduction, copy or transmission of this publication
may be made without written permission.
No paragraph of this publication may be reproduced,
copied or transmitted save with the written permission of the
publisher, or in accordance with the provisions
of the Copyright Act 1956 (as amended).

Any person who commits any unauthorised act in relation to
this publication may be liable to criminal
prosecution and civil claims for damage.

A CIP catalogue record for this title is
available from the British Library.

ISBN: 978-1-80074-716-6

This is a work of fiction.
Names, characters, places and incidents originate from the writer's
imagination. Any resemblance to actual persons, living or dead, is
purely coincidental.

First Published in 2023

Olympia Publishers
Tallis House
2 Tallis Street
London
EC4Y 0AB

Printed in Great Britain

Acknowledgements

I would like to say thank you to my loving family and friends, who have encouraged me throughout my life.

The lonesome maiden:

Finding her beauty, in such perplexity. Standing, upheld with mellow stance. Bare feet, proving her free spirit. Colors and shapes of clothing, matching an instant of purified perfection. The softest of touch, her hand to a carved out cheek. Wondering, seeking her depths prove to be deep. Travels to shallows, seeming bleak. Until now, a forever venture becoming infatuated, with the lonesome maiden.

All to be there:

I've been hurt, and I've been burned. I speak from one, and speak for a few. Many times spent, on long roads to nowhere. Just to gather what's left, and head back home. Love spilled, and fortunes lost. Left with some kind of mess- for the future to clean up. I would rather have everything perfect, but it isn't. Ones heart upon their sleeve, tends to get beaten. But the hurt stands worth it for the one who carries you along. The one who makes it worth it. The one who gives, what you give. The one who cares, how you give. The one who loves, as deep as you do.

Drive:

What drives me: that line, which has never been written. That love, never to be loved. That word, never to be spoken. That taste, never to forget. That sex, so much more than before. That time, never to forget.

Let's be judgmental:

If you don't like my family, I don't like you. If you're a picky eater, you're annoying. If you don't like my music, listen to yours, somewhere else. Don't like the way I talk, speak to someone else. If you're pasty in July, find an outdoor hobby. Can't manage a dirty joke? Melt like a snowflake. Can't swim? Learn!

Country Love:

All I've got to hang onto, are memories of our past. Within my mind, they will forever last. Just don't worry, about where I'm at. Because I'll make it, to where you're at- with you. I've been wandering, with this burden on me. Needing home, and to feel free. Gliding back to you, is all I see. You're my drive, to what moves me. And before we know it, it won't be long. I'll be yours, and all you'll ever need- it's what I feel is meant to be. It's been a longer road, without you by my side. That seat right of me, empty as I ride. Right when it's getting dark, I feel you, and it fills my heart with you. I've been wandering, with this burden on me. Needing home, and to feel free. Gliding back to you, is all I see. You're my drive, to what moves me. And before we know it, it won't be long. I'll be yours, and all you'll ever need- it's what I feel is meant to be.

Bad timing:

It's cold- I'm cold. Nothing left for warmth. It's dry- absent of moist. Cold within dry. I need a drink- when needed most. Water is absent. Food plentiful, when it isn't needed. Not found, when desperate. So many times, what's needed is there. Within the few times, most desired- can't be bought.

Sticks and things:

Your stick, is your sword. Your hand, is your gun. That belt, is your holster. Those sand castles, are your palace. That first crush, is your forever. That rage, is your passion. Those outbursts, are that of expression. Them mistakes, are meant for learning. Harsh words, left for remembering. Ones who die, left with a cry. The distant flicker of home- left lit, for the lost, to make it back.

Coming up short:

The dwarf, on a little horse. Riding within the clouds, on its little course. Neptune to ponder, a little song. Just to be quick, won't be too long. Rides on the winds, of a little due east. Breeze carries bleak, ending within least. Eyes too low, missing sunrise. Ears unable, to hear words of the wise. Rider and horse, seeming too little. Upon this course, not solving the riddle.

Independent Woman:

She glides in, upon a smooth, westerly breeze. Leaving others to ponder her grace. Balancing life's turmoils, as only a woman can do. Providing a mother's sensibility. Never being fickle amongst the little things. Leaving others to wonder what it's like, within her embrace. Coming and going, leaving some kind of residual warmth. The power of success, and being capable of doing it alone. Being capable, of making it great with another.

Times of dying:

Comes the day, the time of drifting away. Not all are ready, for time of dying. Neither those observing passing, nor the one who is passing away. Times like these you think of darkness; not knowing of death. Or moving along to something better, leaving less behind. To the one who's drifting away, and to the ones who are lingering- it's meant to be this way.

The want to work:

Want a better job? Learn a trade. Want to make more money? Work for it. You wanna shine? Wear nicer clothes. You want to impress? Give more than average. It's simple- think deeper, work harder, and act like time, is worth every cent. Be smart- think ahead, as though time is of the essence. Never say that's enough because there's always more to get. Be the king, or queen which wears the heavy crown. Because those with success, carry the heaviest of loads. Loads to which, carry the fruits of success.

Fragmented memories:

Fragments of your memories. Them tougher pieces, harder to place together. As though they're broken apart for a reason. Scattered within the backs of our most distant experiences. Reclaiming misfortunes- those most turbid of times- when you felt the least of happiness, and hurt the most, little by little.

Life's nutshell:

Make money, when you can. Run back, from where you ran. Make peace, with darkened past. Otherwise, it will forever last. Stand strong, when others don't. Never budge, always won't. Forever venture, within your dreams. Goals you concur, always within means. Life fulfilled, when it's over. Creating luck, self four leaf clover.

Tulips through concrete:

Growing where things shouldn't grow. Blossoming within death of growth. Breaking through, when others don't. Finding light, within the gallows. Making fuel, with all the garbage. Laughing out loud, when others sulk. Finding peace, within turmoil. Be the tulip, which breaks through concrete.

Just being honest:

Don't mind the fact, I don't like ya. Not all like me, and I'm one who doesn't like you. It's that simple and let's keep it simple. Let's act like we don't like each other— so there's no confusion. Act as though I'm a bad rash on your ass, and I'll treat you like a bad case of the clap. I'm your itch, and you're my drip. Tell one-another to fuck off. I almost respect you, for showing the fact you hate me. I'll make sure to reciprocate, maybe you'll feel the same.

Just listen:

When wanting to be left alone- telling others to fuck off. When I'm drunk and done, preferring to be by myself. Telling people you ain't up for conversation, but they insist. You say something off kilter, they're the first ones to judge you for it. When I tell you to walk away, it's for a reason. If you decide to stick around, I just don't give a damn about what I say. Being dark, with a bleak sense of humor- not for everyone. To hang out, within drunken gloom, you better be open to anything and everything. If not, do your best to fuck off.

Lovely memories:

I sink, as the sun sets. Those memories, never to forget. One last time, only with you. How I felt, pure and true. Having a night, with you by my side. Letting it roll, letting it ride. No place I can find one like you. Letting it out, those feelings of blue. When I die, we can forever rhyme. Telling stories, of our place in time. In the meantime, I will think and write. To see you again, within time I might.

Old man McCoy:

Old man McCoy, never any joy. From when he was little, just a young ol' boy. Every Christmas, gets a new toy. Just for his drunken dad, to smash and destroy. Never to have anything to enjoy. Old boy McCoy, became a man not to annoy. A man callused, reckless in his ploy. Seeking out, his old man Troy. To his death, a journey void. Never to find peace, was old man McCoy.

Usually unplanned:

Dying behind old, living beyond old. Or right within the sweet spot, where things are meant to end. Like a winter too soon, or a rain too late. Or right within the sweet spot- where things are meant to grow. Like a ship running aground, or never finding shore. Or right within the sweet spot, docking when planned. Neither early, nor late- is rarely the case. Unplanned, takes up the majority of life. Learning to live, as to die young. Striving for longevity, seeking life's length. Bearing the cold, and learning to find quench within drought- that's the majority of life.

Half head:

Half a head, half a smile. Half hanging around, half a while. Half hang, half hard. The last flower on a crisp autumn morning, to blossom for its last time. The last chirp, of the last remaining bird to bear south. The last remaining bearer of fruit giving its last, all it can. Half a bottle, going empty. Half walking around, to stumble one last while. Half hang, half head, for awhile.

Dirt:

We grow in dirt, we water our dirt. We build with dirt, we plow our dirt. We harvest from dirt, we lie in dirt. We work in dirt, we wash off the dirt. Making a living from dirt, we live on dirt. Without dirt, we lie dead in dirt.

Misconceptions:

Sinister some say, with hearts of depth. Not willing to give it all away, comes off as shady. Keeping things to yourself, coming off as untruthful. It's funny- when you spill your thoughts, lay out the truth. No-one wants to hear it. They want you to explain, to lay it out. But when you do- it's judgement, at a distance. People say they want the truth, but they really don't. Sometimes not knowing, is the key to peace. Don't dig, when someone doesn't want you to pry. What lies beneath is usually unsettling.

Close to chest:

Lonely peaks of heightened loneliness. Sharing with yourself, triumph over tribulation. Distancing yourself to an altitude- unable to share the glory- unable to articulate without coming off snub. Weary of sharing, as there are so many takers. As being only a few, down a two-way street. With finding so many, down those one-way streets. Secrets, are best kept to yourself. Success, is best kept within your circle. Happiness, best obtained alone. Once you have it, share with ones, who are willing to share with you.

Whatever:

To walk, with nothing else better to do. Inviting you over, with nothing else better to do. Filling your void, with nothing else better to do. Acting as you care, with nothing else better to do. Ignoring the drama, with something else better to do. Your problems, not something I'll ever do.

Best left unsaid:

Don't ask an alcoholic what they drink, they'll down anything. Don't ask a smoker what they toke, they'll smoke anything. Don't ask a slut what they'll fuck, they'll sleep with anything. Avoid asking someone who's desperate, what they'll do, they would do everything. Don't ask, if you don't want an honest answer. Mind your business.

In the moment:

A bluesy country song- whether to take you home, or to make you feel alone. A winding country road- whether to pay a cost, or to get you lost. A crop-filled country field- wandering them to feel free, or to stay, left to be.

Lack of someone:

Lonely is the path, taken by ones who adhere to solitude. Venturing into where roads become narrow. Lacking the wear of others. Finding oneself, where the path ends. Where no one wants to go. Traveling too deep into nothingness, losing your way back. That's loneliness, that's solitude.

Swaying forward:

Emotions, like a motion, enough to make you sick. Rocking back and forth, on a one manned ship, within the vastness of infinite waters. Unable to control the waves. Unable to steer the current. Vulnerable to ever-changing weather. At times too wet, other times so dry. Once, under the brightness of moon- to be even. As the light- leads the way.

More than words:

Not able to find those words, to best describe my feelings for you. As though language, cannot articulate such magic. As though you're the only path, just having to hope it leads to somewhere. Finding perfection, leaves you with nothing else. Emotion puts everything into their hands, in hopes it isn't squandered. Once in a lifetime, doesn't normally happen twice.

Jagged beauty:

Liking yourself, after a long journey traveled. Not many can say they do. Picking up pieces, learning from mistakes, and creating a mosaic, beautiful within your own way.

Growing of thought:

The wilderness of space, when left alone. Thoughts growing, within all those empty places. Left to grow, without touch. As though time is infinite- left within stagnant void to flourish. Thought left to ponder, without distraction of others. Simple minds, left within simple places. Only able to get deep, by yourself. The simple fact, being unable to relate. To envision words, galaxies, relationships, nuances of life- being able to capture so much, within just one thought. I would just rather be left alone, to explore the infinite possibilities of thought. Capturing gems as they float by. The weight of others, within shallow thought- cannot hold a place, within my realm.

Rough is me:

I'm a little rusty, slightly bent. Got a few dings, and a couple dents. Getting by, paying the rent. All my bills, on time being sent. A little quirky, rough around the edge. Making way, my path I dredge. Willing to work, swinging the sledge. Taking a chance, tipping that ledge. I am myself, and will forever be. Living life, always to be free.

Smokey thoughts:

Midnight watch after a dusk settling on a rusty dusk. Why I must ponder, leaves dripping with wet. Or watching as plants, flex from whither. Adding to fog, with a cigarette. A darkened light, casting from beneath my feet, shadows of clouds, within slow motion. Foot to prop, on an empty chair. Absorbing nuances, not gathered by most. Sinking within the infinity of stillness. Capturing everything, within what seems nothing. Letting go, within stagnant.

Thirsty:

Thirsty when wet, thirstier when dry. The thirst you seek, will never die. Thirsty when woke, thirstier when alone. The thirst you seek, when you're home. Thirsty when he's not at home. Thirstier when knowing, you're free to roam. Thirst you quench, with no-one to know. Never to reveal, your truth to show.

Drunken wonder:

I'm fully drunk, and half tempted to reach you. Not knowing if feelings, of me are true. I sit by the window, and watch the birds pass by. Wondering if, you're with some another guy. Out of all the wonders in the world, you would make a man feel true. And if you're with someone else, you would make this man, feel blue.

Young and Old:

A young man, looks at an old man- thinks to himself, he ain't got much longer to go. An old man, looks at a young man- thinks to himself, he has so much longer to go. A young man, looks into the future- not knowing a damn thing. An old man, looks into the past. Knowing damn near everything. A young man, looking for love- not knowing where to find it. An old man, losing his love- the only one he's willing to die with. A young man, asks the old man: where were you, when you were my age? The old man replies: I was right where you're standing. The old man, asks the young man: where do you see yourself, when you're my age? The young man replies: right where you're standing.

That person lost:

A heightened sense of emotion, leading me to cry. The one I love, laid down to die. The one who got me, the one to know best. Lies to rest, our connection now dead. They say the soul, is to forever linger. Unable to feel it, no longer grazed to finger. Conversation as such, without a filter. Now being gone, left a drifter. Thoughts I compose, only able to write. My person to vent, is gone to flight. Unable to bring, this person back. The stories we told, will forever lack.

Torn through time:

Why my knuckles, are ripped and bent? Just needed, time to vent. Why my palms, are sweaty and rough? They were needed, when times were tough. Why my back, is cracked and wore? After hard work, stiff and sore. Why my head, heavy to ponder? Wonderful ideas, not left to squander. Why must I, manage the pain? It's so I can make it, through the day. What's the path, to your success? It's rough and tough, I must confess.

Forbidden Love:

Grazing your arm, just above my hip. Glancing our hand, almost to a grip. The tension is taught, our feelings prove strong. Seeming to others, our relationship so wrong. Keeping us secret, to dodge detection. Knowing our bond, could result in rejection. My status is single, able to roam. While yours is with someone, waiting at home. Defying my instincts, I press onward. Unknowing of fate, to our love being honored. As time passes on, our bond in question. Predicated on secret, having to hide my expression. Love sometimes found, in all the wrong places. If it fails to pan out, I hope to be in your good graces. The tension so tight, what used to be exciting, is wearing me down, these feelings I begin fighting. To tell you next, this all needs to end. To understand my position, you're unwilling to lend. In rage you cut deep, coming so close. To the destruction of what, I care for most. Once the dust settles, I realize at last. What ended in turmoil, has come to past.

Hiding behind smile:

A perpetual smile seeming so bleak. Hiding behind raised lips, with an upmost protrusion of happiness. We see the brightest of stars, that have died so many years ago. Being fooled by what seems so charismatic. Failing to look behind the veil- dark gallows, that lurk with desponding thoughts- light being dragged to a low. A purgatory disguised with opposition to feelings. What sometimes gleams, isn't always so sheen. What seems so simple, isn't always cinch. At times, optimism is a costume, worn by the saddest of ones. A cloak, to cover up- makeup for some. This one thing, that no one should be good at. Faking dark feelings, and convincing others with illusion. Courage has many forms. One- being honest about pain. Some being ever so stoic- convinced it's right. Failing to see their decline. Many lives have been taken, by ones with their own hand. Who have declined to express, what nobody knows. The fault does not lie with others; it lies only to you, your own.

Loves theory of relativity:

I love to cherish those moments, within depth, within you. Traveling as though, speed of light is too slow. Reaching a destination, never to care of what's left behind. Leaving fragments, for those left to find. Time to exceed slower, compared to all others. To accomplish a lifetime, within a blink of an eye. The greatest of moments, eternity for others. Never to come back, as to what we left far behind.

The mysteries of her lotus:

She shines, she so livens up my life. With a smile so bright, and a body that never stops. I cannot seem to fathom, the beauty of her. The beauty, of her lotus. She's dark, with a mysterious side. As though her beauty and charm, hide a past. A past to which, created her. Formed her. As her blossom, bloomed to a new beginning, to her rebirth. As shown on her skin; the beauty, the scars, the past, of her lotus. To once, to a day. Maybe our pasts, our present times, can collide. To create a future. A future as colorful, vibrant, and beautiful, as her lotus.

Beyond the veil:

I refuse to submit, falling for the bait. Boosting your ego, telling you you're great. Many in line, to grant the mystique. I decline a nod, ending your streak. Strutting around, character so bleak. I see through the veil, your identity so weak. Seeming to others, confidence so broad. Having so many fooled, I fail to be awed. Coming to me, expecting a bow. Shrugging your gesture, I just wont allow. Your face to a glimpse, expression perplexed. Unable to swallow, to what I say next. Enough with the gloat, your ego and relish. What may seem surprising, I am far from jealous. proceeding with reply, you command my obey. Blowing you off, just to walk away.

Natures Wisdom:

These trees stand tall, beginning to speak. As the wind blows stiff, bringing their tones to a peek. The sway of long branches, engaging my listening. Paying close attention, understanding their whispering. Telling a story, of many summer drought. Preceding cold winters, their spring blossoms in doubt. Stoic through time, standing tall to withstand. Hardships through life, are within their command. Forcing a thought to myself, I begin to realize. I'm learning from trees, proving to be wise. Before making the mistake, of thinking you know best. Listen to a forest, that has been put to the test.

Laying my eyes upon you.

Packing my bags, getting out of town. To just be out of reach. The challenge, we yet to see. A step on the boat, to take a look back. Seeing love at first sight, for the first time. You understand why you held out. While laying my eyes upon you- an uphill grind, turns to a downhill glide. Learning your way, as to mine. Finding the straits, of a flowing long way. Making our way out of here. Laying out my hand, welcoming you, to my voyage. Grasping in hopes, taking that leap of faith. Boarding our vessel. Voyaging through, beyond the gates.

Fake:

You're boring- within your own stupid way. Like so many others, latching onto the newest trend. Posting some quote- as if you wrote it. Coming off deep, when you're shallow as shit. Airing your dirty laundry, for everyone to smell- begging for attention. Try being a little more sacred- maybe a quant more mysterious. Maybe you would come off a little more interesting.

Hanging from a rope:

Problems, hanging from a rope. Sorrow, hanging from a rope. Troubles, hanging from a rope. Worries, hanging from a rope. How easy, is hanging from a rope? Thought to ask, the person I saw hanging from a rope. That question I should've asked, before seeing him hanging from a rope.

Deeper thoughts:

Seems almost morbid- the mortality of time. Life fickle, only taking a moment to smite. What one takes in, leaves a little behind. Certain things so easy to obtain; others not. Certain things so easy to lose, others not. The future at times, fragments through a prism. Life with infinite directions. The guidance of wisdom, only for the fortunate- or for the ones seeking it. Death to a nothingness end, or a new beginning. Levels of intuition- only captured by few. Herbs of this planet, taking you to where you're meant to be. Love, as to being the most powerful entity within the universe. Thoughts with no textile- having the most substance. The singular point of being, to the singular point of end. How small can something be, before it's nothing. How big can something be, before it's infinite. The mind cannot grasp certain concepts. Concepts which might exist. Let's think together and solve the universe.

High times:

Another line, to another toke. Filling the room, breathing to choke. High as hell, ready to blow. Beers going down, easy it's flow. Out of mind, blurry my sight. Crash to burn, at the end I might. Mind going places, within other dimensions. Warnings obscure, many failing to mention. Clock moving fast, at other times slow. Not to freak out, staying in the flow. Experiences from one, to another bloke. A mind always sober, never removes the cloak.

Shelby:

Shelby, as sweet as a 65 mustang. On a hot day, like a drink of tang. Booty too fine, ain't never quit. Moves to kill, her sway so hip. Lips taste, of strawberry wine. How can a woman, be so fine. To a glimpse of her, walking away. Hoping to see her, on a glorious day. What makes Shelby, worth the ride? Those moments in step, with her to stride.

Isolated in thought:

My mind works better, when I'm alone. So many people tend to limit you. Shackle your potential. I can go places alone, where I can't go with others. That's the beauty of the mind- being able to think and do anything, on your own. Most are boring, nothing they bear brings new thought. Latched onto what's popular, what's proper. It's either they refuse to go deeper, or they can't. Unable to relate, within my peers. Finding yourself to be alone, among groups of people. Finding yourself wandering off, away from the chatter- to explore, within yourself. Imagining things, that only you can.

Scars:

Scars- I have accumulated over the years. Some worth talking about, and some not so much. Some scars to show stupidity, others inflicted by others. Some were by accident, and some were required. Scars for family, scars for success. My scars are plenty, from unwilling rest.

Never again:

I've seen her black eyes, too many of times. It's a story, I've heard too many times. Always her fault, something she said, some kind of random thing she did. As though protecting the one, who doesn't protect her. And sometimes, her matters fall into your hands. When you do something about it. Just to do it by yourself. Never to tell a living soul. Taking care of the problem, so the problem goes. After it's done, seeing her eyes glow. Without a hair, or thread out of place. Knowing she'll never see, another monster again.

Safe and lonely:

I don't deserve much- at most, I deserve myself. Lost, within the trinkets of time. Buried, within the hardships of love. Worn, within endless work. Finding no energy, to give to another. So many lost opportunities because I couldn't find the motivation. Lost in work, lost within myself... as everything I care for, melts away. Building a wall, just to keep everyone else out. Unwilling to commit, in fear of being hurt again. Finding solitude to be safe, yet lonely. Lonely is the life, lived safe.

By yourself:

I have fun, by myself. I drink, by myself. I smoke, by myself. I think, by myself. I write, by myself. I have found myself, by myself. I create, by myself. I invent, by myself. More things should be done, by yourself.

Dusty times:

Cracked dirt, hardened clay. Sands to split, in dryness of day. Where clouds never cry, never to drain. Scorched is the place, never to see rain. Blistered feet, wandering heavy. Tears rolling out, breaking the levee. Perpetual weight, strapped across back. Long the voyage, on this hardened track. The only thing now, is where I stand. Becoming one, and dying with the land.

Words of advice:

Even if she looks like her mother, ask if they're sisters. Asking a friend out for lunch- pay the tab. Be the second, to walk into the room. Throw a dollar, in the hat of someone playing guitar on the curb. Seeing someone struggle- at least offer your help. Hearing someone's bad day- don't be the one-upper. Call your mother, try as hard as possible to fulfill plans, and never tell someone's secret. Take gossip, as a grain of salt. Only trust, ones proven to be trustworthy. Always shake with a firm grip, and look eye to eye. Strive for goals, one by one. Know your limitations, and always ask for help when needed. Don't act as though you're the smartest in the room- even if you are. Talk to the elderly, like an adult. Treat a child as though they're grown. Give advice, only within your scope of knowledge. Save your credentials, because no-one gives a shit. Live how you wanna live. Love who you wanna love- and die without a dime in your name.

Problems:

Some have drinking problems. Some have smoking problems. Some have coping problems, and many have life problems. Your problems, are shared by many others with the same problems. Problems of yours, problems of so many.

Isn't always so:

Let the club do the work. Let your money work for you. Just let it rest, leave it to simmer. Turn the other cheek. Take the high road... The club is only as good as the one swinging it. Your money only works, if you work for it. Letting it rest, is putting it off. Leaving to simmer, only becomes cold. Turning a cheek, is backing down. Taking the high road- well, sometimes it requires a back road.

Complex:

What hurts, and what feels good- is what you do to me. Compelling, yet sometimes boring, is what you do to me. Sometimes thriving, and sometimes dwelling- within happiness, and pain. Seeking a mind complex, is the complexity of finding it. Complicated, yet simple. Is where I find myself. Wanting simple, and complexity- is the challenge. Rather live alone, than to share unhappiness. Not to do me any favors, by sticking around. Willing to linger, never to be found.

A night out:

Let's dance around, a center of romance. Unknowing of last names, not giving a damn. Lust, feels like love- when you dominate my lonesomeness. Feeling as though you're everything, everything I've never had, and always wanted. Luck runs hot, through to morning- when the smolder, becomes a cooling ember. Our love for our lust, melts away- as the sun shines, on a new day.

Trip to the Gulf:

The sun blossoms through a cloudless dawn. The shadows of palms, just whisper the tides of the gulf. Tropical creatures, stretching out the rust of sleep- as myself, having conversations with mom, of how we're going to capture this perfect day. As the shine hangs noon- walking side by side, without casting shadows. Sharing long, sugary beaches within oceans of nature. Lying on a sheet of warming sands, darkening through the afternoon. Once the sun dims it's light, making way for evening festivities. When people are happy, drunk, and free. Dancing as though, it's their last day. Singing amongst those, who strum guitar, drink local booze, and drag off cigars. Making friends, with total strangers. And living life, how it's meant to live. After all is done- making a nest on a cozy balcony. Letting the sounds of the gulf- drift me away.

We've all been there:

Fishing for a compliment, talking about your shortfalls. Wanting a pat on the back, by explaining all the work you did. Asking for feedback, after a night of cooking. Looking for advice, when you spill it out. We've all been there. Maybe wanting more than you deserve. But hey, throw a bone- give a word of bold, say how hard it must've been, compliment the dinner, and give whatever advice you have.

The Moon:

The moon, always true. It's scars, to never change. It does what it says it's going to do. It's full, when it's supposed to be full. It's crescent, when it's meant to be. It's harvest, in the fall. Has no atmosphere, no protection. It takes the hits, over time. Over the years, still hanging within the void. Always there, when you look up. Never to cower, never to hide.

Dead ends:

Killing myself silently within the acts of impulsive nature. To be asked, by one, of good nature. All I can say is no- with some pathetic excuse. Running from the better things, to drown within the comfort of normalcy. Companionship is known to be needed yet, finding yourself within lonesome thought thinking about it. The desire to break free, lacking the energy required. Sitting, resting legs on an empty chair. Knowing the answers, unable to conjure its motivations.

Take care of things:

If you plant a flower, water it. If you own a pet, take care of it. If you have a job, earn it. Find someone in need, help. Making more than you can spend, share it. Someone asks you for a bite, share it. First at the door, let the person behind you go first. When someone shares, listen. If they wanna be left alone, walk away.

What inspires me:

Love, life, loss- to name a few. Feelings, feuds, fortune- for a couple more. Nature, nights, nuance- is where I find myself. Sleep, slumber, solitude- to get me going again. Time, thought, turmoil- can make it dark. Sun, shower, sex- feeling of bliss once more. What inspires me? A lot of what inspires you. To name a few.

Better now than before:

Older now, looking back to when I was younger. A better man now. Worn a little, looking back to when I was newer. A better man now. Piled mistakes, looking back to when I had fewer. A better man now. Fewer friends, looking back to when I had more. A better man now. Looking back, from where I am now. A better man now.

Healing within view:

Taking a look in the mirror, for a better view. Stabbing an untamed glare, to tell me what's true. Filling the cracks, with a trek through the void. Alone in the room, seeming to tell I'm blue. Healing the scars, in ways not a clue. Learning with time, making it through. Heal, by taking a look in the mirror- for a better view.

Taking chances:

How crazy was he: he tested experimental parachutes, he ate, what is now considered poisonous. He climbed the tallest of mountains, without a net. He used his hands, without a safety clip. He flew, when no one has never flown before. He gave everything, with no guarantee of return. He sacrificed, when no one else would. He's that rare breed, not found quite often. Found only within search. Found only within truth.

Find a true you:

Peace lies, within narrow boundaries. What's wide, so unfortunate- is the un-rest. Clashing, as so many do. Unable to mingle- not able to see it through. Among the hard heads, exists an ignorance. Few now-days, can soften up to others. At times, finding yourself within a wasteland. The ones you encounter, unable to articulate- unable to understand- seeming so dull. So many people, are wasted- caught up in what's cool- caught up in what's hip. They venture further away, from themselves. At the end of the day, there are very few real people. Just a bunch of puppets- being coursed by others.

Give a little:

What drives me crazy- when people compare their hardships to others, and minimize those they do it to. Rather than beating us to death with your plight, take into consideration the plights of others. We all have ups, downs and hardships. Rather than keeping score, let's try giving out some points.

Random night:

8:14- a purple pink sky. Just till tomorrow, this day come to die. Down of the sun, leaving brisk. Cold to touch, just a fingertip. East shines light, onto the next. Within the meantime, I'll grab some rest.

Just for yourself:

I get drunk with birds. I get high with squirrels, and I make friends with toads. I talk with my cat, and stare at the stars. I find beauty in nature, and comfort in lonesome. I prop my feet on a hair, that isn't filled. I eat prime cuts, cooked for myself. I buy expensive things, just for oneself. I grill for taste, when nothing else matters. I take long trips, just for myself to flatter. I work long hours, within many days. Always changing, upping my ways. I burn oil, to keep nights lit. To keep that fuel, a writer's whit.

Live a little:

Ever ride too fast on a motorcycle? Or drive like crazy in a sports car? Ever feel the wind in your hair, without a helmet? Ever fly first class, on a 40 minute flight? Have you tasted champagne, from a 600 dollar bottle? Or eat Louisiana oysters, fresh out of the gulf? Ever drop a few, on a fantastic night out? Or treat a woman, to a fancy opera? Ever be an extra, within a movie? Or act a fool, within a long night of groovy? Or invest life savings, on something flimsy? And end up rich, when others thought was gloomy? Life not lived, on the edge. Can leave you short, falling off the ledge. Take a risk, have some fun. Before you know it, all will be done.

Lend an ear:

Listen to those in pain, who are willing to share it. They're giving you their time, by asking for yours. Don't shy away from hard conversations. Never be afraid to dig deep. Always look close, when others gloss over. We have all helped another, without knowing it. And we've all hurt someone, without realizing.

Alien:

I'm an alien, from outer space. Sometimes unable, I struggle to relate. I cast my gaze, about this place. Wondering these people, the human race. Wanting to love, sharing within embrace. But all I see, is hate and disgrace. I think I'll fly, my way back home. Keep to myself, until harmony unfolds.

Real men:

Real men cry, mortal men die. Men ask why, with tears in their eye. The working man gets by, reaching for the sky. After a long day applied, letting out a sigh. Let a man fly, rather than sulk and lie. Leaving a man dry, after saying goodbye. Let him try, his devotion to provide. Just be an ally, not asking much for a guy.

Spare me:

Today turns tomorrow, you make me a promise. That we will spend time, your lies become chronic. To get my hopes up, telling me our plans. Doubtful it pans out, I leave it in your hands. Juggling the date, to when you'll finally come around. Seemingly hot to your hands, the idea falls to the ground. Rather than pick up, the remains of our plot. I assume let it lay, leaving it to rot. I begin to grow leery, frustrated and aggravated. Beginning to think, I make you feel obligated. Spare me the favor, of promising your presence. Feeling as if desperate, the thought so unpleasant. The need to move on, I have found in reflection. Our paths moving forward, in opposite direction.

A dog named Ned:

Once knew a dog, name was Ned. Built like a mule, with a boulder of a head. Paws as big, as a grown man's fist. Not a hound, you wanna see pissed. But Ned had a heart, one of gold. Ned was a dog, one worth known. He would lick and snuggle, just before bed. Listening to books, his owner once read. Ned was a gentle, friendly old dog. Snored like a train, slept like a log. Ned loved his family, through and through. A dog's love, is pure and true. Throughout his last days, Ned was weak. But still stayed strong, for moms love to keep. Ned was wise, like a ripe old man. Maintaining the keep, until his final stand. When laid down, for his final rest. His love will stand, lasting the test. When stories are told, of big ol' Ned. Only pleasant words, are left to be said.

Truth - the new taboo:

Let's circumvent the truth. Let's crowd the line, waiting for the comfort of lies. Let's sugar-coat what needs to be said, just to save face. How about we blow smoke, to avoid hurting feelings. Let's act not ourselves, to fit within all the boring others. Let's just stay shallow, avoiding riches within the deep. I'll just act like I enjoy you, dreading every minute of it. Let's smile, behind our frowns. Never to speak, of what troubles you. Let's hate pineapple pizza, because social media says it's nasty. How about we make no sense, because it's politically correct. Let's refrain from truth- the new taboo.

Do what you wanna do:

Eat your steak well done, drenched in ketchup- because that's you. Talk to yourself, when no-one is around- because that's you. Smoke those cigarettes, and drink that beer- because that's you. Act your kind of weird, and be yourself- because that's you. Walk at night, in the pouring rain- because that's you. Not to give a damn- living your kind of life- because that's you.

Simplicity:

What's your drink? Anything. What's your favorite food? Everything. What works you up? Not much. Who's your kind of people? The ones worth being around. Who do you trust? A few. What gets you out of bed? The morning. What temps you? Something intriguing. Who's the smartest person you've ever met? The most simplest of ones. When is it not your business? When it doesn't affect you. When do you leave something alone? If it isn't worth being messed with. Why is it so complicated? Because you make it that way. Why the drama? Look in the mirror. Can you be happy? That's up to you.

Good old age:

Just a bit, long in the tooth. Like an old tree, showing its roots. Ripe with age, bares most ripe. These younger youth, wound too tight. Just to melt, like a snowflake. This younger youth, the heat they can't take. Leave it to age, to show the way. To not lose faith, for chivalry to stay.

The blues train:

I ride the blues train, when I'm down and low. A little less rough, when down and slow. On-aboard, when feeling the glow. Hearing that whistle, howl and blow. My next stop, I don't know. Let this train, tug me in toe. When it ends, don't seem to care. Where it takes me, I'll manage the bear.

From a man's heart:

Let me grill, I'll feed you forever. Let me make money, I'll pay the tab. Let me spend time with buddies, making it up to you. Let me drink, for a fun night out. Let me be myself, to give you what's me. Let me hold, in time of need. After a long day, lay me to breast my rest. Allow me to bitch, until there's nothing left. Let me be a man, the man you need.

Then it comes:

You're my star, that I think will never burn out. Then one day, it does. Blinking deep in the sky, and one day- within a blink of an eye, you're gone. Your light, I could always see- turns off. The rivers that flowed, between you and I- within darkened night, runs dry. The talks between you and I, sometimes ending with a cry. Another cry, I would give, for you to be alive.

Coming together:

The older heart I fond for- that lonely heart- seeking re-new. Within a young soul, I can't remain- they just lack the old stuff. To the old rhythm of blues, or the grim of grunge- That's my domain. I enjoy hearing a life spilled out- of defeat and triumph. That's a life well spent. And as I hear your blues, within rhythm we connect. Lord knows, you can't change your world. But I can bring myself, within your universe. And maybe you and I, can create something true. And maybe if we could, change the course of our worlds.

Those ones who look perfect:

My fingers look like a mangled mess, because I'm a nervous wreck. My hair is perfect, because I have to make up for it. I've got perfect teeth, to hide my frown. I've got a toned body, to hide the inside. I drink alone, to hide my feelings. I'm sober with others, to wear a mask. I extrude confidence, to hide my insecurities. I tell what's wanted to hear, to avoid conflict. I ride on legend, because it's all I have. To act the hammer, feeling like the nail. Leaving trails in sand, for tide to wash over. What seems to be, never real.

What I would give for my sisters:

What would you give? Everything. What would you sacrifice? It all. How much time are you willing to spend? Eternity. How much money? Every penny. How much love? My heart. How much of yourself? My soul. To give them vision? My eyes. To allow them to hear? My ears. To give them hope? My happiness. To give them guidance? My way back home.

It's that simple:

When I call, I wanna talk. When I don't answer, I'm busy. When I'm tired, I sleep. When I'm content, I'm awake. When I love, I care. When I'm done, I walk away. When I say it, it's what I want to be said. When I'm quiet, I don't wanna talk. When I drift, I wander. When I'm home, just wanna stay still. When I'm relaxed, I seek comfort. When aroused, I seek pleasure. Simple- can be the essence of life. To fill a need, is all you can do. To ride with feelings, is staying true.

The way one holds:

You can tell a smoker, by the way they hold a cigarette. You can tell a drinker, by the way they hold their liquor. You can tell a liar, by how they hold promises. You can tell how someone cares, by the way they hold you up. You can tell compassion, by the way they hold your heart. You can tell the strength of someone, by the way they hold themselves together. You can tell everything there is to know about someone, by the way they hold things.

Just the way it is:

Some have it all, and deserve nothing. Others have nothing, and deserve it all. Some get lucky, with no train of thought. Others strike out, with full head of steam. Some strike gold, with nothing invested. Others lose it all, betting everything. Some dodge guilt, with life spent badgering. Others suffer grief, with life lived honestly. The mystery of life is such- beyond reason, beyond explanation. Good people get hurt, and bad people can thrive. Life isn't designed, to always be fair. It's designed to be random, beyond rational contemplation at times. All you can do is plan, react, roll with the punches, and ride the waves. Life seeming random, as it always stays.

Do whatever:

Roll me up, or roll me away. Whatever you feel, however you may. Pick me up, or set me down. Either left stranded, or to be found. Feelings felt, or not so much. Fingers to stray, or palms to touch. Crossings paths, or going separate ways. Either way, making way through the day. Spare the favors, of showing me love. Not my brand, not my kind of fun.

Have you ever:

Have you ever been drunk, in a pouring down rain? Looking at nothing, and seeing everything? I have... and it sucks- but at the same time, brings a sense of knowing. Have you ever listened to a song, that brings you down? But you need it, to think about what you need to think about. I have... and it stinks- but at that moment, brings a sense of comfort. Have you ever smoked too much, lighting one off the other? Craving one before the past one done? I have... and it smells- but I like it, and it keeps me content. Have you ever thought of yourself, burning from both ends? Thinking you're selling yourself short? I have... and it lingers- and I keep doing it, knowing I have an end.

Questions:

What do you consider deep? because I'm deep. What do you consider weird? Because I'm a little weird myself. What do you consider late? when I stay up all night. What are you ok with? When I'm ok with everything. What keeps you up? When I'm awake. What memories do you keep? When I spill away. What lingers long? When I'm long away. What keeps you faithful? When I don't have faith. What keeps you around? When I'm not there. What keeps us apart, is what we don't share.

A looping dream:

Looking upward, while lying over a forever, dug out dredge. On the bed, staring at the ceiling, again. Once I saw it, over a tipping, drawn out edge. Out of bed, never to ever, wanna see it again. On the floor, my legs to a race, they bend. My dream calls to say, before I wake to day. As I roll out again. There's the reason, clouded by dream, and snow bound cold. Once again, I wake up out of bed. In a field, lost again. And then, I can feel it. The waking edge- all in a dream, not being real. Confused in sleep again. And then again, I can feel it. Right then I know, again- never to understand.

Changes:

Riding down an old long road, by myself- with no one, alone. With nobody, why so? Maybe my ways, coming off a bit cold? Could be time, for a change. So many times, regretting throughout the years. Could've saved, so many tears. Down a journey, of long patchy road. Bearing regret, feeling it's load. Riding down an old long road, by myself- finding my way home, alone. With heavy thought, why so? Changing my ways, coming off a bit warm. Embracing this time, for a change. So many times, never seeming so pure and clear. Having yet, so many years. Down a journey, of long patchy road. Bearing strength, in future to hold.

Regrets:

Found a couple notes, from the good times. They were so sweet, with your silly ol' rhymes. Found myself thinking back, on the good times. Wish I could've, seen the signs. Found a bottle, from the old times. Tastes bitter sweet, of your fine wines. So I sit back, with a cigarette. And think about, my regrets. And yet it's ok, sulking in my own pain. Because you're here, within memory to remain.

Rock Bottom:

Same old shit, and nothing new. Looking through clouds, seeking some sort of blue. On the cusp- of rock bottom. Wandering around, in gloomy fog. Gotta wonder, how I get around. And still it stays, circling rock bottom. Spending nights, in a gritty gloom. With no lights, in a darkened room. Barely afloat, reaching rock bottom. Turning thoughts, to something new. Like the thought, of being next to you. Pulls me away, from rock bottom. My same old thoughts, that have come to be. Melt away, when you're next to me. Can no longer reach, rock bottom. You finding me, on brink of bottom. With drunken breath, and emptying bottles. I can't count the times, you've saved me from being rock bottom.

Backroads:

Long stretches of dirt, feeling like home. A long drive, when wanting to be alone. Either by foot, or in my car. Traveling its distance, not to wonder how far. Steep curves, to snaking bends. Following the path, wondering where it ends. From sloping fields, to prairies of grass. A long drive, slow to last. My mind, free to flow. Getting back, to those backroads.
Trouble is...
You drink too much. Smoke too much. Have too much fun, and sometimes are unprofessional.
I work too much and sleep not enough. Coming off, maybe a bit rough. Maybe a drink to get by, or a smoke to get high. Whatever your vise, to get ya by. Humors too dark, reactions too gritty. Such a foul mouth, and responses too witty. Bitching too heavy, outlook so gloomy. Showing up to work, with an attitude too groovy. Whatever your mood, we're in it together. When times are tough, bearing the weather.

The fickle of life:

Orange flowers, within glossy fragments of time. Seeming awake, just to awake. Rolling clouds, within darkened gloom of sky. Seeming alive, just to live. Raging heat, within chilling cold of night. Seeming warm, just to be bitter. Dimmed dawn, within forecast of morning. Seeming to begin, just to end. Staying awake, from night to the next day. Seeming early, just to be late.

From dream to closure:

Insomnia, lies in between loneliness, and dream. Unable to drift from solitude. Unable to reach you within slumber. When I finally venture into your void- within sleep. I am then awoken, to what it's like, with you. What I thought, would be more than I could imagine. Ended up to be, a frightening tail, with you. I then awaken- happier than I've ever been, without you.

Two of a kind:

Two happy faces. Two of different expressions, two of different colors. Two with wings, two with dreams. Two of infinite possibilities, and futures. Two being different, two treated the same.

Short half-life:

Talk how I want, say what I want. Not giving a damn. You find it offensive; I find it funny. Not all, get the dark side of this humor. Make fun of you, make fun of me. If not, what else do we have? My nights are darker than most, and I'm ok with that. I'm off the cuff, random, and weird. Sure beats being normal. Losing some, speaking my mind. Gaining others, doing the same. If you don't like what you hear, or see. Do your best to fuck off.

Missing out:

Always catching me, within a blink. Always missing, what you think. Approaching me, within a mood. Coming off, edgy and crude. Eyes open, fighting sleep. For a talk, for a meet. When I'm up, you're down. Sinking in this, falling to drown. Always too fast, or too slow. Never finding, an even flow. When it's meant, never to be. Gotta leave, gotta be free.

Don't:

Don't leave me with hints, or things left unsaid. Don't trust what you hear, or everything read. Don't walk away, when it isn't done. Don't drop it all, in a dead run. Don't change for some, and not be yourself. Don't break under pressure, keep true to you- and all it's wealth. Don't dim your light, when others are dark. Don't stand quiet, when others won't bark. Don't stray, from who you are. Don't burn out, keep fueling your star.

Rhythm and soul:

Dark glasses, with a slouched groovy style. Hearing the music, knowing I'm staying awhile. That riff on guitar, a lot of groovy. With drink and a smoke, my spot feels roomy. That rhythm drum, with a bluesy beat. God this bands, packing some heat! Four drinks in, more to come. Music so good, unleashing some fun. Old base, slapping with fingers. Those bellows roll, feelings to linger. That keyboard man, mellow and cool. Pecking away, and that singer, sulky with some gloom. Brings to life, a crowd to bloom. Can't beat some fat, rhythm and blues. Playing to the soul, sounds so true.

I need a little more:

I need a little more social, I need a little more rub. That good kinda rub, that kind from love. I need a hobby, not your normal run. Not the ones, that everyone else does. I need a place, for my own kind of fun. Within that moment, a place to run. I need to lay off, the smokes and rum. Play it straight, some clean old fun. I need to settle, for some steady. Not running so hard, burned out and sweaty. Needing a choice, between two roads. Feeling comfort, within the way I go.

Where I'm found:

You'll smell me through the breeze, and find me in the sky. Freedom lifting from my wings, as I cast wake, soaring as I fly. Only one way to look, in your search you might find. Casting gaze to up, leaving the ground as you climb. You can't teach work, you find it in a stare. Looking in the mirror, finding it in yourself, within a glare. Only in darkness, one can find the light. As tough as it is, learning how to fight. Learning more from down, than from being high. Learning how to swing, maybe I fall, maybe I fail- I might.

Me for you:

Asking me to warm up a cold night, I can't. Asking me to bring the aroma back to your wilted flowers, I can't. Wanting me to talk differently, or walk less swiftly- I don't think I can. Telling you what you wanna hear when it isn't the truth, it doesn't seem like I can. But to ask me to change, just a bit, just for you... I think I could.

Too late:

Good advice, telling him to not go all-out. Advise too late, damage already done. A black and white still, of a man smoking a cheroot. Leaning against an old Ford, flathead V8. Within it, of ripe old age of 28. He'd be lucky, to make it another decade. A life full of sin, catches up quick, to be paid. So don't tell him, what he should've done. Where were you, when it could've been done.

Simple answers:

One sometimes contemplates the universe, and all the facets to this life. Solving the world's problems, one drink at a time. Thinking of a million dollar idea, to just forget it in the morning. Solving hunger, by stumbling to the fridge. Ending poverty, by waking up for work. Ending hatred, by being friendly. Not feeling so lonely, by inviting over a pal. Wondering the vastness of our galaxy, by accepting that you can't. Finding happiness, within what you have. Ending envy of others, by focusing on yourself. The worlds issues, within the ever vastness of the cosmos. All those questions answered- by just looking in the mirror.

Summer bliss:

Sitting in fields, lying so green. Seeming as though, living within a dream. Your wooden chair, made of oak. Brings me life, a blink of hope. Lavender blossoms, smell within bloom. Draw me back, from a place of gloom. Lines of trees, bank the crop. Walking within your fields, begs me to stop. Summer of bliss, always to shine. A feeling so rich, a feeling so fine.

Drinking into darkness:

It's so hard being drunk around other people, when you're so used to being drunk by yourself. Getting over shit. Seems to be the hardest thing to do. Hoping in the morning, forgetting what you've been through. Falling asleep as snow falls on your head. Thinking of thoughts, that can never be seen through. Freezing within time, within mistakes, that will forever last. Never to wake, within a ventured journey. Thinking about less and less, as the bottle goes empty. Zoning out, off into the blankness of what's in front. A burning cigarette brings you back, as it burns your fingers. Dinner for one, drinking for two. Ink runs dry, after writing a few. A one way trip, for some, a bleakness into forever.

The night before Christmas:

12/24, Christmas Eve. Santa's gifts, left under the tree. If you wake, if you might, to see Nick's cheeks, rosy with delight. Leave a cookie, leave a note. To Santa with love, the story she wrote. As it starts, written with soul. Asking what it's like, living in the north pole. Why his beard, is bulbous and white? And how Santa's sleigh, takes off in flight? Why his suit, velvety red? Not a stitch out of place, perfect each thread. How do you fly, to all in one night? Leaving presents, before it gets light? I do believe, in Santa so real. Eating my cookies, with milk his meal. As morning comes, I failed to wake. Sleeping until he's done, is Santa's fate.

Romantic Geometry:

Our thoughts for each-other to correspond, to a heightened altitude. The angle in which, the light shines through your hair. The center to which, we can relate. Hitting our chords, our harmonious rhythm. Here and there, to be together we coordinate. Feelings for each-other, within heightened degree. Distance between us, never too lengthy. Love for you, can never be measured. Finding those moments, within our medium. Our thoughts to run, forever in parallel. Few to understand, around the perimeter. Our light to color, through the prism. Within your touch, beyond proportion. Inside this realm, sharing your sector. Fitting together, to make whole our segment. Marveling our shared, pronounced similarities. Giving this vision, beyond true clarity.

Deeper ideas:

A deep mind wake, from a dream done. Words he hear, sounds a bit of fun. Most to scatter, in a flat out run. Deep mind peak, to shine in the sun. A dreamer's dream, to others none. Casted out, others to shun. Few can say, they're the one. After days done, to say they've won.

Curbside:

Come have a drink with me. Alone, alongside the curb. When those bars close, never lining up, with your end of the night. Crack a beer, light a smoke. Let's talk about A, and through, to the very end of Z. Let's watch that sunrise, with what little we have. That little bit, of what we have- meaning so much. Doing our thing, as only we can do. Conversations, only kept between us two. Giving my little bit of dark, and casting your little bit of light. When we depart, we shall always stay. When we come together, feeling as though we never left. Along the curb, along with you and I.

Shuffling through time:

Seventeen, one year ago, I drove to school. Five years in the future, drinking my first legal beer. Six years before that, getting drunk on nine rolling rocks. Three years forward, smoking a crackling cigarette on a pizza delivery. Ten years prior, catching my first frog. Rolling back another three years, falling off an un-saddled horse, breaking my arm all to hell. Shortly after, my sister bringing me home trick-or-treat candy. Twenty-one years later, I start my career. Ten years looking back, writing my first poem. Fifteen years later, writing this, 11/9/2020.

Traveling the cosmos:

Time spent with my mind being within the stars. Too much time, spent away from home. No-one down here, to understand what is to be seen, up there. Mind-bending connotations, traveling through the wormholes between galaxies. Finding myself so far away, from everyone else. As though my soul must exist, within another time. Time other than the present, is where I lie. Lying to myself, as though I belong. Relating to unworldly beings. Finding connections, within inhuman things. Intertwining with black holes, quasars, and the heaviness of neutron stars. Gravity pulls me away, from where I stand. Pulling me away, to the stars. Spending my time, away from home.

It's done:

When she comes to you with a problem, you take care of it. When a friend needs your hand, you drop what you have in it, and give it. When your mother asks for more time, you carve it out. When a sister asks for advice, you find it. When your neighbor is out of town, you tend to their flock. Within yourself, needing more? You work. It's simple- for ones you care for- you give everything.

All in this together:

In the lines of black, and of blue. In the end, we're all being bruised. Common ground, not seeming to be found. Drowning out each other, messages without sound. What's good for me, and good for you. Never to rise, never to come true. Giving in a little, the same in return. Listening to each other, so much we could learn.

Saturated:

The time is darkness, 0107. My ways can never see brightness of heaven. Some say I drink, and smoke too much. As though I must drink and smoke my crutch. I can seem mean, smelling of ashes. It's just me, screaming my passions. To nose I'm pungent, of aged whisky. My mood stagnant, lingering and stinky. Times such as this, best left alone. My grunge in demeanor, etched into stone. Catch me when binging, seeking the truth. Life not lasting, not to seem long in the tooth.

What it must, will become. Digging deep, not to circum. Passing time, foot to stool. My thoughts to ponder, my mind to fuel. Deeper than most, brain so heavy. Wanting most, not to break the levee. Few can understand, thoughts I carry. The depths uncertain, comprehension will vary.

Playing your tune:

The beauty of pecks, from a piano. Spouting my words, the beauty in you. Riding into solo, from left to right. Voice to peak high, on important chords. Callous, building on the tips of my fingers.

Working so hard, on the prettiest of notes. Playing out, ending my tune. Melody to hear, bouncing off the moon.

Observations:

Spider webs, across the grass. Only to be seen, though a setting sun. Leave the spiders be, and the grass to grow. Leave to be, before the snow.

Vises:

I've been on the camel for too long. Starting to feel a sense of drought. That same ol' feeling, with each passing day. So I light up, the natural, American spirit. Hoping maybe, for a better taste. Wet the whistle with Modelo- seems to be a pattern- in regards to its translation to English. Tomorrow, maybe a Budweiser. But E, never comes before I. Maybe in a sense- I, needs a drink. E- every time, making a change- exchanging, for the same damn thing.

Why we work:

Wind to blow, the smell of dirt. Under the nails, a stench of work. In the fields, working the plow. Whatever you do, sweat to brow. CPR, to cleaning the floors. Working for a living, earning what's yours. Fitting pipe, to pounding nail. Assembling parts, or throwing bale. Whatever one does, dirty or clean. Coming home tired, not always sheen. After a shower, cracking a beer. Why you work, becoming so clear.

How geese fly:

The one in the front, cuts the wind for everyone else. After awhile, moving to the back for a break. As the next one in line, takes its place- to cut the drag, for everyone else. After a long journey, each one, sharing the load. Who said you couldn't learn a life's lesson, from a flock of geese

Blind love:

Blind, left with only touch, and feel. Eyes black to ponder, could it be real? Asking once- for a view, to see that touch. Dark is the view, my sight is the crutch. Hands to caress, to envision I must. Love and appeal, within you I trust. Guiding me to you, lending your hand. Telling the truth, as where I stand.

The impossible:

As though, I'm climbing on clouds. Or smoking a broken cigar. Riding a bike, with no peddles. Or catching a fish, without any trebles. Making it, to where you are... as though, flying a kite, without a string. Or shaving my face, without a blade. Making my way, with no direction. This climb for you, seeking perfection.

Putting it out there, unable to take:

Laying it out there- expecting as though, it won't be treaded on, critiqued, questioned or judged. So many find pleasure in judgment of others, unable to take it from others. Throwing stones, while being so fragile. Laying it on, unable to bear the weight. Your course of action leaves a tread, for others to follow. What you seek, within venture of speech and action, leads to a destination. Expect others to follow, and be there- waiting to give it back.

Loving what you cannot have:

Looking through brightness, blinded by the light. Knowing deep down, that something isn't right. Casting my gaze, hoping for notice. Your blooming flower, the beauty of a lotus. Pink and white, the colors so gorgeous. Like a harmonious tune, sung by a chorus. Repeating your tune, that so many have heard. I dare cross the line, that seems to be blurred. My feelings towards you, are not a deception. Hoping you see me, behind your reflection. The courage is high, so I ask the question. If the feelings are mutual, I wait for your confession. Turning your gaze, you tell me so gently. My feelings towards you, are not beyond friendly. As I digress, my heart is broken. Your words so soft, so softly spoken. Composing myself, preparing for response. The words I cannot find, unable to pronounce. So I drift back, to that moment in time. Where my thoughts of you, were so sublime.

We're all guilty:

We've all been let down. But don't feel too bad for yourself- you've let others down too. When you're feeling betrayed, led on, and ridden astray- always know, you've done the same. Don't react in a way, like you've never been guilty, of doing the same. When one lives long enough, they lose the ability, in ways to condemn. As though the act taken upon them, they have never partaken onto others. When you're lied to, know you've lied to others. When mis-spoken to, remind yourself of how you have treated others. Mistakes being made by one, you've done the same. Keep it real- keep an open mind. Remember how people have done you wrong. Remember how it made you feel. And remember, how you have done the same. Because those dark feelings, you have inflicted on others as well. There's no better way to learn. Reflecting on what has hurt you, and realizing you're guilty of it.

Solitude:

The crime of solitude. As it's so addictive. It's separation, from the heavy burden of interaction. Interconnection within a world, dictated by oneself. Entertaining thoughts and self-exploration. Without having to worry about amusing others. Within the me time, neglecting others. Finding comfort within loneliness, as forgetting the warmth of being with others. Finding it being easy making yourself happy. Excluding the ones, who could add a deeper layer of contentment. A cozy rut, of solitude. With giving it enough time, can isolate you forever. It's this back and forth, of human nature- having to be alone, and needing someone else. And finding the balance- tending to both.

Already been there:

Can't rattle me, I've been rattled loose. Can't shake me, I've been shaken too many times. Can't break me, I'm already broke. Can't keep me wondering, I already wander. Why worry about you, when I can ponder about me? Telling me I should change, when what I do is me. What more can I lose, after everything is gone? What can I ask for, when nothing will ever change? Nothing to drink, when the well is dry. Nothing to eat, when the bone is bare. What more can callous, over hardened hands? What a soul can bear, after a life of wear?

Desperate nights:

There's gotta be a hole in the bottle. Otherwise, how have I drunk so much. Seeing a gorgeous woman, drink the last, of a last pour. How poor a man, to drink once more. Keeping up, that bill to pay. Being the man, to drink once more. How deep the bottle, is my bill to pay. Feeling the debt, as I drink once more. A long drive, is the risk I take. Paying the debt, to a drink once more. Making it home, drunk, is to which I made. Luck, as to a drink once more... and so it goes.... to a drink once more.

Myself:

You're right; I don't talk about myself. It's myself, and I like keeping it that way. Like when I'm alone. Listening to what I wanna hear, and thinking about what I wanna think. Keeping it that way. Not trusting anyone, because the one I trusted, is now gone. It will always be that way. Riding high, for myself to enjoy. Sulking low, for me to endure. My highs are for me, my burdens are for me to bear.

Living like an idiot:

Up creek without a paddle. Telling her to calm down. Taking up that offer for a cheap hooker. Riding out that stream of sting. Jumping that gap, you know you can't clear. Driving a long way, on a low tire. Taking gaze, of that solar eclipse, waking blind in the morning. Drinking too much, too late, having to act normal in the morning. Telling your boss to do their best to fuck off. Buying sushi at a truck stop. Thinking you can hold it until the next exit. Thinking an oil change last 80,000 miles. Leaving that shoe untied, because I'm too damn lazy. Eating spaghetti on a first date. Falling in love, too fast. Thinking you know someone, before you don't. The odds are in my favor, to crash and burn again.

Start to finish:

Finding yourself at the beginning, looking towards the end. Seeming so far and long from the present. Head down, feeling the saturation of time on your body. Eventually, looking back to the beginning. Seemingly so close and brief from the end.

Sometimes in the fall, it speaks to you when you're alone. Without a face, without a name. Just a chill and a breeze. Once in awhile, stopping to not talk to myself. Letting what's around, do the talking. Slowing my walk to lesson the noise. Eventually coming to a stop. What I find on stony gravel, within the most darkest of nights, is silence. Silence which speaks. Telling me what's needed.

The guts wisdom:

The ramble, of a siren. Loud, is it's tone. It's ripples fill my gut. Telling me, the truth- that has to be known. My mind trickles back, putting my senses at ease. Learning, in the course of time. My gut, is how it has to be.

Ambivalence:

We can all meander through life. Living in the middle of the road. Never veering to turn, or take the rougher road. Always staying on the interstate. Never taking the scenic route. At times, rolling the dice. Taking a risk. Betting so much, on something so uncertain. That's living.

Regrets:

Perhaps a miss-step. Within lack of judgment. Yes, talking about myself. Spitting words, cutting like a knife. Stating exactly how I feel, without thought, of another's emotions. Lacking care, when that's all, that was needed. Walking away, when I should've stayed. Embracing what I had, before turning it away. Cutting someone short, before they could really explain. Ending the night, before one was through. Throughout my entire life, I have made mistakes. But in doing so, taking from it. Trying to recapture those moments. So I can replay them, again. Again, with the mindset of the past. Acting as though, I give a damn.

Discipline:

Sometimes, there's nothing more, than a little less. Shrinking your world, to only what's necessary. Tunneling the mind to just look forward, or up. Find a star in the dark, and refrain from plucking it from the sky. It's so much easier to just look at it. Or attempt to untie your shoes, before taking them off. Having to tie them back up in the morning. It's a discipline- not always trying to take too much, or lacking the effort, to save a good pair of shoes.

Voices of no end:

On a long, drawn out voice- taking me away. Along the causeway- down the road. Taking me up, to the highest embankment. As we descend low, to the waters, of your cross way. Taking the long way- finding it hard to understand, why I can't stay. Like a long, drawn out swim. With ever sinking depths, and forever, drawn-out shores. Casted away- drifting amongst the waves, of your drawn out voice.

Losing it:

Just seeing it's light, for the first time. Knowing it burned out, some time ago. I was there, when the light spawned. At its nucleus, to witness its genesis. Must not have known, what I was looking at. Walking away, as I did. Walking far enough, to no longer see the light. As it sinks in, realizing what was lost. I then see, it's light. For the first time. Knowing it burned out, some time ago.

Robbing to pay:

Taking too much time from tonight. Leaving too early, of a morning. Robbing the night, and short changing the day. Waking tired, from hours awake, after dusk. Just being too close to daylight.

Fun times:

Plenty of light, bumming a smoke. Slurring in speech, I'm drunk- he spoke. Music is deep, feelings it pokes. Nothing to hide, bellowing with folks. Solving the worlds, infinite problems. From world peace, to who should wear condoms. Laughing as though, there isn't tomorrow. Putting away our lows and sorrow. As for tonight, a love-fest with cheer. Problems we have, we don't wanna hear.

Speed of light:

Traveling at speeds, exceeding light. In search for answers, to make it right. Maybe this truth, will bring you, it might. Not always quaint, not always polite. As though, just for once, maybe just tonight. To hold you close, embracing you tight. Read you my love, for you I recite. Just not enough, having to rewrite. Maybe a spark, a poke- to a bite. Something spontaneous, fuel to ignite. Acting as though, your canvas is white. Hiding your flaws, living in fright. Show me your colors, vibrant and bright. Whatever you are, will be alright. As we glow, scorching the night. Exploring our romance, at the speed of light.

Awakenings:

Deep within sleep, to awaken- rising out of entrenchment. Still to hear, the residual voice of god. A message conveyed, by the all mighty- as though it's holy message was only meant for you. In awakening- deciphering the hallowed code. Contemplating its gravity, it's unwavering, precise, to a pinpoint demand. How? You ask- how can one, such as myself, carry out such a monumental task? Beginning to question- was it, what I heard, the voice of god? Or maybe my inner subconscious, within myself? Maybe I'm more, than what I thought? Maybe I'm deeper, than this shallow muck? This muck I find, within myself. If the voice, was that of divinity- I can understand it's weight. But if the message, came from within- I have to question, what I need to change. Sometimes truths that are hard to hear, and the hardest to carry out- don't come from others, or from a higher power. They often come from within. And it takes the strongest of people, to admit when they're wrong- when the message is right.

Yellow-stained mattress:

Upon the sheets, a soaked-stained, withered out bed. Having to explain these yellow stains, again, he dread. Waking frightened from dream, his body lay wet. Explaining why, is what they'll never get. A life being scared, shown on his mattress. Discolor of torment, disdained, scorn in fabric. Making fun, of a boy so stressed. Unable to help, within sleep, to make a mess. Only one wish, the boy prays so deep. For fear not to take over, and drown him while asleep.

Legacy:

I want my legacy to be left, upon the foundation, to which I built. A legacy of working hard, and sacrificing what was needed, to leave behind something, to which I'm proud of. A legacy of helping others, reaching out, and obtaining goals, by going through the grit. Coming in early, and staying late. Spending time with someone who needs it, when you don't have the time to give. Lending help, before helping yourself. Giving up your last sip, or giving away your last bite. Sharing two, when you only have three. Doing something so inconvenient, because it's convenient for someone else. Legacy not only encompasses yourself, but how you gave, and sacrificed for others. Not just embodying self-achievement, but achieving for others, who couldn't do it for themselves. There are times to take, and there are times to give. And knowing when each is appropriate, creates a truly good legacy.

Is what it is:

Lucid and translucent dreams illuminate such vivid imagination. As though my night's sleep, brings to light; a heavenly existence. Not one, which seems to germinate within our soil. Why such rich fields, never seem to spawn- a genesis, a beginning. Such paradox- having foundation to grow, waters to yield. Never sprouting through. It isn't me, it isn't you. Maybe you just lost your feel, for me. So let's just leave it be because it seems we can't see eye to eye. It isn't your fault, and it ain't mine. It's just you and I, and we just disagree.

Learning through time:

I can't tell you how many times I've fucked up or have said the wrong things. In anger, wanting to say things that cut deep. Being the most uncaring prick, to ever walk the planet. Acting as though your existence doesn't mean a damn thing. Telling one to fuck off, to walk a long hike, off a short peer. All these things, said within a rage. Unable to take back, the spoken word. Unable to digress, from my fits of rage. I get it, I seem to learn, from the darkest of times. Real learning never seems to happen, when you're acting your best. Seeming as though I have to be my worst, to realize the good. The good, that I am. Ones seem to judge you, on your darkest hours. Find the ones, that see the light, within your brightest of moments. But don't take advantage, of those wonderful souls.

R we forever:

Revolutions- as my mind spins for you. Rabble- disorderly thoughts, to where I stand. Rabid- are my feelings towards you. Racket- as to judgment in loving you. Raconteur- telling our story, as being so interesting. Racy- our times together being so exciting. Radiant- as to your beauty. Raffish- not all will agree. Rakish- in that low cut shirt, and high cut skirt. Ramble- for hours, finding words for you. Ramification- of this love seeking truth. Ramify- growing together. Rampage- setting forth, to accomplish everything. Ramshackle- life without you. Rancour- if it never works. Random- is our carried out plan. Rankle- which will never be. Rant- of needing you. Rapport- is what we have. Rapt- totally in you. Rarefied- only by you. Raring- to give this a shot. Ratify- to our commitment. Rationale- to keep moving forward. Raucous- exclaiming our connection. Rave- for you, which I can only speak. Realm- wanting to be with you. Rebuff- I can't do without. Recalcitrant- not going with the flow. Recant- never to our feelings. Recapitulate- reminding you of how I feel. Repartee- sly speak to spice it up. Reticent- to which I felt before. Retrogression- never within our lives, together. Retrospective- how I lived before you. Retort- our thoughts so witty. Risible- laughing until we hurt. Rider- telling you, it's going to be alright. Rift- rolling through our struggles. Riposte- lashing back. Risqué- as to my behavior. Robust- efforts, making our way back. Roughshod- not considering your feelings. Rudiment- getting back to basics. Rue- regretting my behavior. Ruminate- thinking of myself, to change. Rummage- for the answer. Rigmarole- troubles now, our resolutions to come.

Burning from both ends:

Wanna lose weight? Switch to liquor. Need a stress relief? Smoke tobacco. Happy with your weight? Keep smoking tobacco. Feeling the need to let off some steam? Have wild sex with a complete stranger. Seeming to have the urge to live it on the edge? Ride a motorcycle without a helmet. Wanting to live 100 years? Avoid my words of advise.

Cindy:

I'm my thoughts so breezy. Within glimpse of Cindy. Wide eyed and teary, the mind flighty and windy. With flowing hair, and a woman's eyes. Can't seem to sleep, no matter how hard I try. All alone with me, I wait through the night. To imagine our love, taking flight. Regardless of time, approaching to morning. In light of you, alive my adoring. Wide eyed and dreaming, my mind flighty and windy. In my thoughts so breezy, within glimpse of Cindy.

In the stars:

How fast can I travel, to reach the stars. To reach this love, where you are. Looking up, at your dot in the sky. To give everything, for the ability to fly. Seeing you, only at night. Like within a dream, shedding your light. What I want, not here on earth. Searching regardless, for what it's worth. Coasting through day, waiting for dark. To see that speckle, your light, your mark.

Memories of past:

I miss my papa, our times spent. Where the time goes, wondering where it went. Sitting back, drinking wine. Man those days, forever to be fine. Always him, for words of advice. Thinking back, tears swell over my eyes. Long nights, of stories and laughs. No longer there, those moments to collapse. Telling his stories, of distant past. Moments I'll cherish, always to last. When he left, after he died. A piece I lost, I can't deny. So as I write, as I cry. Thinking of the man, such a special guy.

Having your back:

Take it easy, take it slow. Strap me up, let me lighten your load. In this together, down this road. Paying that debt, a debt owed. Helping me, and helping you. Keeping it straight, keeping it true. Veering off, losing track. A pat on the shoulder, bringing me back. Hard for you, is hard for me. Your troubles are mine, is how it will be. Bringing me up, when I'm down. Always knowing, you'll be around. Having to fight, standing your ground. At your back, is where I'll be found. Never to lose, sharing our struggles. When push comes to shove, we'll bloody our knuckles. Breaking it down, at the end of the day. Together we stand, always our way.

Day Eight:

After a long, dark and dreadful seven. There will be light, on the eighth day. The day after seven, which one cannot find, in a book, or on a calendar. Day eight exists, within the mind. That one day taken, for oneself. This day, only belonging to you. On the eighth day, all one has, will be lighter, and rejuvenated. The stresses and fatigue of the first seven, seem to melt away, on the eighth day. Eight, being infinite. Unmeasurable possibilities of fulfillment. Starting from, and coming back around. Filling the prints you made in the morning, with spruce feet, after the days done. Let's ride, stroll- sit to ponder, and go with the flow. Be selfish, be kind. Do what is you, and at sunset, unwind. Stand alone, or with a friend. Revel on your eighth, before doing it again.

After death:

A soul, rising from the depths. Upon the moment of death, leaving the soul no choice. Not knowing where life goes, upon last breath. Either sinking within the soil, or soaring with wings- upon a blinding light. Or maybe choices, poorly made, sinks one beneath the glory of the light. To burn, in scorching heat, throughout eternity. The only ones who know, are the ones who experience that moment, beyond living. Unable, to tell the living, of what's next. As though death, draws everything within the abyss. Death, as the event, over the horizon. Never to be known, never to be seen, again.

Red Bird, Red Bird

Red bird, red bird- tell me your secrets. Far beyond pleasure, and those of bleakness. Dig though thoughts, tell me your past. Of black and of color, how you've mastered your craft. Commitment you found, within shallow youth. With age, on becoming, finding your truth. What was right between two, so long past. As time withered on, feelings didn't last. Seeking new, as growing older. Finding new spark, new love to smolder. Cuddling at night, hidden by darkness. Pleasures we seek, shine through a varnish. We talk, we pry. Unveiling the truth. Hard on the case, senses of a sleuth. Interactions reveal clarity, of our deepest feelings. One has to question, the reality of leaving. Looking back, on such a long past. Happiness varies, on a journey so vast. A question remains, to leave, or to stay. In hopes that love, will find its way.

Drawing you:

I seem to be having trouble with the eyes, and her hands. I cannot seem to capture their beauty. Limited within my talents. What I put to paper, doesn't justify what I have seen. Maybe another pencil, maybe a slightly lighter shade. Maybe I should run my finger, through her hair. That may be, what it needs. Fade that dark, into a more flowing light. Her chin, possibly obscuring the jaw line. That ear, cutting off that line, which pronounces her neck. The drawing of an eloquent neckless. Not too far high, but never too low. The cut of her dress, has to be perfect. Just far enough to show the top of the knee, yet leaving curiosity to be wondered. How about her heels? No more than three inches, no less than two. Their straps, must show the foot. Crossing over the top, just showing the delicate nuances. With a proper nail polish, to go with the outfit.
As I draw, I draw you. That last night spent, with you. As only memory can re-create. As time passes, all I have, is pencil and paper. So I struggle, to regain connection. As you were, how you are. You will forever be, my lonely art.

Sharing our love:

I have many friends: from all walks of life, and of many races. Ones who are white, black, Hispanic and Chinese. From Greek, to Iranian. Russian and Japanese. They each have a story- of struggles and triumph, from hearts broken, to a healed soul. Ones who have crossed borders, and have dealt with hardships; and ones who have helped, the others, through their darkest times. Looking back, on all the people I have met, and the ones who I have grown to know. We all have torments, turmoils- just different, within our own ways. What I have found, within my journey- is to pick people up. No matter race, beliefs, or creed. When we all help each other, everybody rises. Rather than looking, to the color of skin. Look deeper, within the heart. Learn people, and what drives them. Their motivations to sustain life, and relationships. Beyond the cover, lies many pages. Just take the time, to read someone's story. We can have differences, and learn to exist, with each-other. Respect my opinion, and I'll respect yours. And maybe someday, we can find a common ground. Where lush grass grows, and happiness is found on trees. Where rivers flow, surging with love. Eating at my table, and eating from yours. Sharing with one another, the fruits of life. Maybe one day, we can all break down, what divides us. And come together, surging towards the future, together.

Together and apart:

Love runs deep. A relinquishing feeling, that it can cut even deeper. Love can so exist, between two people- but to forever fall, within the abyss. The meeting and growth, of two people. Can start like two peas, tightly woven, within their pod. Eventually, as though time withers away your seam of bond. To then end, in ways seemingly miles apart. This I have learned: love, being the most unstoppable force within the universe. As everything eventually dies, love can forever burn. It can nurture, swaddle, pull one from the depths, and lay ground for an incredible future. With everything, within its infinite ways, has no guarantees: love can bind, love can bend. Taking one to a brink, until they break. Love can shackle. And rip your beating heart, right out of your chest. Love can be, the gift that life gives you. Or the curse, to forever torment you.

Eloquence of you:

As eloquent, so fluent. On a soft cascade of eloquence. May I must remind you of the soft suede, nestled between your soft skin, and a velvety surface. One's soft words, whispered upon a soft ear. Light touches, being laid upon tender skin. Rolling ever so smoothly, beyond ones fingers. Lay upon me, a touch so delicate. Remembering once more, a time so eloquent.

True North:

Always north, of what faces you. Mistakes made, lessons you grew. Never let past, dictate your future. Allowing your present, to be much smoother. Always trust, within yourself. Because all you have, is within oneself. People gab, people talk. Just do you, and strut your walk. Act from passion, as if it's only what's left. Never fail, as life, is the test. Just be true, to what you know. And everything else, will work out in flow.

Drifting in thought:

Driving next to a train, going in the same direction. That feeling of majestic, nostalgia. Very few I feel, can recognize this feeling. As though you're hanging off a rail car. Dirty, and smelling of past. Departing, from what you're leaving, with no idea where you're going. The ultimate sensation of freedom.

Hardened memories:

I live hard, harder than most. Drinking, to follow a smoke. Not to gloat, not to boast. Reaching the line, hands off to coast. I've aged, beyond my years. Riding fast, and sulking in tears. Few can reckon, this journey I've rode. From heartache to booze, so steady it flows. I may die, short of many. But memories I have, are far beyond plenty.

Lusting urges:

Minuscule, within a vast temptation. Ones thoughts, seem to linger with one, and not the other. Minuscule, to some, but not others. Talking, with tongue of lust. Just the same, as sharing the same bed. Lingering thoughts of provocation, straying you away, from what you've committed to. One who ponders, with dabbling- to dabble, in entertaining. Wandering away, from your homestead. One must question, the quality of home. Before you linger, before crossing the line. Ask a question. What do you need, compared to what you currently have? Happiness, in many ways, selfish. Having to focus on oneself, in order to reach it. Sometimes having to stray, in order to find it. As though supplementing your current life, with another person. Leading two lives, because the one currently, doesn't fill the void. What isn't found at home, found elsewhere. Always work, on all of your relationships. They require maintenance, upkeep, spices thrown in. Don't always look at the perpetrator, as the only one at fault. No one ever knows the story, behind a closed door.

Savoring moments:

One must luster, fragments of life. Otherwise you're left, with feelings of strife. At times, making mistakes, within opportunity for love. Pushing it aside, giving it a shove. Things wanted most, within life. Sometimes take second chances, an opportunity coming twice. Before moving on, giving it the shoe. Look what you have, what's in front of you. Sometimes chances, don't come twice. Realize the risk, of rolling the dice. Love I have lost, fault is my own. Opportunity slips, opportunity blown. One thing is left, within my quest. To learn from mistakes, to do my best.

Fickle my feel:

This mood is fragile. Like old glass, tempered with age. Like the pelting of sun, on an old, withered fence. As though the flicker, of a flapping moth- could wave a hanging, shred of cloth. The chirps of birds, a breeze through the trees. Quiet one seeks, silence to seize.

Lonely peaks:

A tempered state, within dark glosses of fade. Cloaking a darkness, feelings long made. Casted by light, still within black. Unable to shine, through a slim crack. Hated by most, feared by many. Unable to count, the number is many. My climb of the mountain, to its heightened peak. Others who spit, with thoughts so bleak. Success is sought, by so very many. Few take action, the rest are plenty. Grit, work, guts- to make the climb. To so very many, to its voyage they're blind. Before you rest, and ask for a hand-out. Think of your pride, your work to be stout. Focused, like a laser, shutting it out. With full steam ahead, plowing your route. In seek of favors? Words of advice? Your fate lies with you, earning the prize. From here, take action, intensity within your eyes. Without the guts, your dreams will die.

Avoiding the past:

Time creeps in, as a sensory of perception unfolds. As this time entails, lessons of learning unfold. One wants to linger, within a past, that no longer exists. Relinquishing love, which no longer prevails. Asking for one, another chance- met with a wall, built to block, the fury of your past.

Clear:

Something ain't right, right now. Giving yourself cheap for a ducket. Feeling better because you did it your way. Giving yourself away on the self-agreed term of what you have to do. If anything's going to bring you down... it's going to be nice, bring it down with you by my side. As for me, trying to describe your truth without sounding so hurtful; as keeping it to the waist side. As what you think matters, really doesn't. What sounds so sad, isn't so bad with the ones of the same plans. A crowded mind, clearing way for clarity... making way, for your way. Like the streets of Broadway, making room, for all willing to share their story. An ear to hear, and an eye to cry... understanding your road, as I walk your streets. Without a judgement to give, or advise to preach... tracing your footsteps, as only you can make.

Cyclical:

Time, sinks, within a deep void. Unable to move forward, nor back. Stuck within a place, maybe within your mind. Of dark solitude, as everything else passes over you. A drag from a smoke, a slurp of a drink. Unable to shake, thoughts that I think. Taking in, what's been told to me. Analyzing, each and every facet. Figuring it out, just to do it again. As a bat, blind, finds what it needs. Wandering, with arms out, unable to let it be. So, to a smoke, to a slurp. Salute to ones, feeling hurt.

Something more:

Moreover- as a further matter, besides the one, which lingers over my shoulder. Through-and-through in every aspect, completely encompassing my thoughts. As though being the case of something deep. Whereas in something as contrast, as to what I see. In light of seeking knowledge, for my own consideration. Thereof, as my declaration is pronounced. Whereas- contrasting to my statement. Incognito- it's truth ever so concealed.

Playing the fool:

A man so thirsty, unable to drink water. Why? Is the first question. "I hate to say, so long ago, water drowned me. Almost to a point, of no return." I ask: "What water could bring you to such a brink?" The man replies: "Water so deep, which I trusted to its very depths. Water seeming clear and pure- full of life." Replying with question: "What lurks in water so pristine? Seems as though pearls and jewels would float to its surface. As though flows of love, in a purest form, would soak one's body. Able to bask forever along its surface." The man replies: "Its waters are so deceiving. I found this shore just upon chance. I fell in love with its upmost perfection. As I treaded further within the tide, feeling water go from my ankles, to my waist. I've never felt so at peace." Within upmost anticipation, I ask: "What's next?" He then continues: "As I floated, upon waves so soft, something I couldn't see grabbed me, and dragged me towards the depths. Its grasp was soft, yet vindictive. I told myself to resist, but I couldn't. As though it sensed my feelings of bliss. Taking advantage of my ambivalence. Before I could think a rationale thought, It was black." In obvious confusion, I reply with the question: "How did you get back?" With reply: "As though my soul dragged me from the murky depths. I found myself ashore. With scars to prove, a scheming voyage. What brought me back, alive- I can't seem to explain. As if fate, lended a tugging hand. My love for its waters, gone. My trust of its beaches, broke. What lurks beneath it's gorgeous surface, something dark. So oblique." In thought, I reply: "What such metaphor, can explain a fear so great for water?" He replies: "This thing I speak of, under disguise, is a love I fell for. As of now, unable to drink; as being so thirsty. It takes, only time, to heal the wounds from beneath. And one day, maybe one day- I can drink the waters once more."

Passive through:

Passing over, so it seems. So many approach life as such. As though something coming, is better than what's present. A lot, as it is, wasted. Passing over trinkets along the way, hoping for so much more at the end. Within a view of my own- pick up, and savor those little trinkets. It makes sense, to be only natural, that one will be richer along the way. And if one reaches a deep well of fortune; it's as though one seals with a cap, a full and fulfilled venture. Furthermore, if one finds that the well is dry at the end- there's always the quench, of the past, to make it through.

Jon Withers:

Jon Withers, as he waits for death. Withers is the name, of what's left. Lying on a bed, that has slept so many. Taking the lives, their souls so plenty. A multiple of people, gathered around. Waiting for Jon, to be absent of sound. This man lay so weak, but his mind still wise. Holding strong, until the moment he dies. Before last breath, gazing stare into eyes. The ones he loves, stare as they cry. Hold the hand, of old Jon Withers. Give the warmth, of love through your fingers.

Round Window:

Looking though, a rounded window. Just cutting off a sliver of your face. That piece that shows the good side of you. The other side, seeming to droop. What's seen, on the other side. A face, just cutting off a sliver of what's good.

Love, and all its torments:

Love, and all its torments. For someone who spills words, just can't find the right ones. In anger, words that cut deep. And unable to reel them back. Just to explain, it wasn't meant what I said. Lashing out, from a source of self-frustration. Trying so hard, so desperately to convey that it isn't their fault. The fault, which is my own. Wanting in desperation, a companion. Unable to be there mentally. Some of the greatest things, just have the worst of timing. Gripping ever so tightly, as loves water can't seem to be held within your hands. Watching it flow, away. Never to be seen again. Time heals, they say. But time doesn't fix what has been broken. It can only close it away, within some dark cabinet deep within your mind. Always to be broken, just closed away. It only takes one time, not to break something fragile- such as love. I can only learn, from the fractured pieces of what once was. Maybe in time, fixing what is broken.

The place of Forrest Crest:

Just beneath the border, of life and its stress. Lies a quaint little town, that of Forrest Crest. A land of peace, with milk and honey. A place of tranquility, stuff not bought with money. Lying on sheets, made of flowers. Just getting lost, in your thoughts for hours. Mind finding peace, within its land. Not a worry to care, its own special brand. Where people care, and lend a hand. Or to be alone, soaking the sun to a tan. This place so real, within my mind. Until I wake up, leaving it behind. As I sleep, within Forrest Crest, my mind can wander, as I lay to rest.

Lost in today:

Watching and waiting, for delivered to become read. Living life on your phone, one might as well be dead. Glued looking down, as life swiftly passes. The addiction so real, while observing the masses. Snapchat and Facebook, Twitter to reddit. Many moments lost, and much fewer who get it. Remembering the times, of face to face talk. Strolling down the road, or getting lost in a park. Life and its luster, not found on a phone. Take a look up, and life's riches will be known.

Storms of the mind:

Wind blowing stiff, breeze turns to blow. Bringing thoughts from a flight, breaking to a slow. I ponder what's life, and where I am meant. Wanting what's high, fearing my descent. Worry so real, anxiety turns to doubt. Expelling my fear, feelings turn to shout. Cascading emotion, for what I want most. This fondness for peace, wanting so close. Tipping towards forever, towards the abyss. Longing for pleasure, in the fields of bliss. My mind playing tricks, shackled from free. Pleading for sovereignty, for power I plea. What will it take, besides seclusion. To figure out, this storm of confusion. I dare to let out, this thought I fear. Emotion so real, sheds to a tear. All I need, is a shoulder to cry. To let it all out, emotions to dry. Worry so silly, what seems to most. Don't feast on the host, vulnerable and exposed. Like a tick to lime, disease to spread. Carrying the sentence, leaving me for dead. What seems like for most, life laid back. My worry to fracture, spilling through the crack. Seeking to fix, this condition so tiring. Observing no care, that thought so admiring. One day in hope, to find the pleasure. This happiness I seek, to fulfill and treasure.

Rocks to ware away:

To weep tears, onto a shoulder cried on so many times. Like a rock, a wall to lean on, finding comfort, which can soak hard times. Soak them to dry away, anything heavy on a mind. A vent for consoling, an ear for listening, a voice to reason. Not to realize, in so many moments past, that this one thing, will not last. One day, having to find a new shoulder, another rock, or a sturdy wall. As if trying to find water, within an infinite drought. To quench a thirst, within loss, that seems to sprout. What was real, now a memory. What was once embraced, merely within a mind's mirage.

Moving forward from what's behind:

Typically in life, there's more to what's coming, than to what's already happened. Living within stride of running, from what's behind you. What's behind, can never change; nor, can never replay again. Slow down- take a moment to digress, and move on. Move forward slowly- as time never stops. Embark on journeys, knowing they will end. Saver those moments, and do better tomorrow. Better than you did yesterday. As life's a journey. One, which requires mistakes and misfortune- for one to really grasp the moments, is one who's lived through those moments. Moments of which, are different. Different from the ones experienced now. Different from moments coming. Never judge yourself, based on the past. Learn, change, and move on.

Moon nights:

A thin sliver of crescent, on the lower right half of the moon. It's full potential, outlined within a darkened shadow. Look up tonight, change the pace, of always looking down. We can all enjoy, tonight, a thin sliver, of our neighbored moon.

Swift and slow:

Glimpsing, a drifting foreshadow of thought. Once it enters, so swiftly. Just to drift away. Sometimes things stay longer, slower than its approach. Leaving quick, or leaving slow. Other times, creeping up, like it's lasting forever. To linger, making one ponder- so lethargic, with its departure. And sometimes, hitting you like a truck- it's lasting effects linger- or to swiftly wither away. Approach, slow, fast. To linger long, or to never last. To leave, so quickly, or to forever stay.

Only within a dream:

Once upon a time, staring into your eyes. As the sea turned to a light, sparkly blue, upon a sloping horizon. Your scent blows from a swift breeze; grazing my nose to a flare. Finding my face to be weightless, as I cast a marveling stare through your hair. Communicating through emotion, as only our toes touch at the fringe of a foamy tide. Unable to wrap sense around such an exotic moment in my life. Feeling as though a false move, or a wakeful jolt, will arouse me from this fantasy. Waking to an unfortunate reality, as our love exists, only behind closed eyes. Maybe as I lay, closing myself away, I can find you amongst those waves. Toe to toe, drifting my way back to you.

A crooked old bend:

A crooked old bend, grown over with lifetimes of foliage. Not traveled so well. No footprints to track, or a trail marked. Only a smudge, within a thickened wood. Very few have traveled, fewer to push through. Life in a way, a metaphor displayed-within nature's thickest layers. What's great, seeming at the end of a lifetime of travel. Few embark, on a crooked old bend.

Warm memories:

Take me back to that place. Where so many of those loving memories were left behind. Hoping that the gust of time, hasn't carried them away. It's been so long ago. That place so far behind. What is left- a foggy, fragmented memory. Wanting to re-trace my steps from the present, back into the light of the past. This place so warm, so rich. In thought, realizing I can only reminisce. Only able to feel a distant, radiating warmth from the past. Lost, in the distance traveled.

Darkened past:

Hardened callous, not to give a shit. Of what you've seen, or what has been done. I tread, wearing out my own soul. Witnessing a cheat, or a lie. To not give a damn, till this life run dry. To you, to everyone, to which I think. To a whiff, makes me think- this shit stinks. A long dirt road- after three days of rot. A 357, head blown from a shot. Memories from when, I was young. Hanging from a tree, a man once hung. Shackles nailed tight, to an old wooden beam. Names carved in wood, victims fall short of dreams. Childhood maimed, by memories once lead. Thoughts to linger, rolling around in my head.

Natures feel:

Rolling, as it seems too long on a winters tail. Chilly is the night, shallow into May. Ahead, unknowing, as plants are planted, and yards are mended. One chill, of a frosty eve. Can kill, everything tended. One must feel, the freeze of winters past, to grow, a springs yield. A soft finger, on nature's pulse- learning its rhythm, like tree to moss.

Reminiscing:

I look forward, to the past; to become the present. As long days, seem to wither thin- wanting to relinquish with a step back. In thoughts of complaints, of yesterday. Seeming so small, as of today. Shops to close, and to cover your face. Makes one long, for yesterday. Starting the day, with thoughts of dread. Looking back, when it was different. So many tread, on such darkness of days. Wondering its end, for the past we pray.

Limitations:

The certainty of mathematics; which I can't seem to wrap my head around. From one, plus two, equals three- to the theoretical physics of life, beyond what we know. Created by people, which could never understand. In theory, which they say. In other words, not able to contemplate. We are one, within millions, those, within billions, among those, within infinity.

Interactions:

Scrolling through the pages of others. Listening to sounds, that I would like to change. Lighting up a smoke, as a means to an end. Slurping on drink, flowing to relaxation. Moaning of a mood, which seems so oblique. Laughing off response, as though not effected. Observing, with blank stare- a deep sense of thought. A slight left of the chin, trying to analyze another's thoughts. In means, of diverting attention, from the observer. Sometimes you have to look away, to see what's in front of you. Trying to think, where I've heard this verse. As you speak, trying to interpret your words. Only the one, you say. But seems so many. Mellow and dark, sings the tune. It's like you're running, into forever. Reeling you back, back to unknown. Letting you go, as it should be.

Towards the end:

Why so stupor, on such heightened level. Your mellow, seeming so low. As my charisma, leveling so high. Where can we meet? It's forever, to be unknown. As a piano plays, I dream of you. To picture our emotions, running through. So open, to your flow. I only dream, of your stream. I'm in awe, of your memory and what you meant to me. Forever your light, will never fade. Towards my dark, I have to prevail. There is no choice, but to move on. In glimpse of tomorrow, one must, carry on.

Eventually mixing:

The least you could do, is to develop a mutual understanding. How I feel, and how you feel and how that correlates. What melds with me, can it possibly meld with you? You rush, as I slow. You ease, and I resist. Sometimes, it's not ok. But not always, with you. I try leveling off, with you. When it shows, so unsteady. Towards the end, it melds. As we mix, it seems to fit. At its end, feeling ok.

Natures Evening:

A bullfrog in the mud. The dragonfly balancing on the end of a fine-tipped water weed. Metallic Mallards bobbing for what's beneath. Feeling my souls suctioned to the chilly muck. The sun at its highest point. Casting not a shadow of myself. The still, glossy surface of the water penetrated by a hungry fish, pecking at a drifting piece of leaf. This backwoods stogy is starting to burn short. Each drag gets a little warmer between the thumb and index. Rolling smoke, over the back of my shoulders. That dragonfly found something else better to do. Those metallic mallards didn't find my sneeze attractive; and that fish must not like leaves. Sitting in this creaky chair, realizing all my companions have left. Flicking that drawn-out smoke into the water, is ending my day. Forgot about the bullfrog. There doesn't seem to be a smoke small enough for that big fella.

Riding it out:

A sense of tranquility, upon choppy seas. Within order of serenity, riding rolls of emotion. Remaining within stillness, as everything seems moving. Composure, order- rolling with unsteady. Wrap me within, a place of placidity. Riding out this storm of obscenity.

The loner:

A lonely whistle, never heard at noon. Only amongst night, shadowed by the moon. He sings and ponders, alone within the night. Hiding his wallows, never to see light. Among judgement, dark in its gaze. Traveling dirt roads, set in his ways. Talking with no-one, only within himself. Always comfortable, alone to himself. Thoughts to flourish, like a breath of fresh air. Without a worry, without a care.

Getting to know:

How deep is ones river? Floating on its surface, unable to glimpse the depths. The unknowns of depth, of bends, of its choppy currents, to its ends. One can only drift. Neither a guess, nor an assumption, can determine its true extent. To know it's curves, breaks, banks, and ripples takes time, rolling with the drift.

Voyage of Courage:

A rolling number of times, is what you see- crashing to shore, as each break takes away a little more. Wanting so desperately to set sail on high tide. Risking waves, which could sink your vessel. Counting days, which seem weeks. Finding within yourself a will, which never prevailed before. A will to sacrifice yourself, in attempts of finding yourself. A mind being isolated- it's patch of island, within an ocean of everything else. Feeling each ounce, wasted away. Knowing time will never be exactly right. Reaching down, to finally cast away. In drift, seeming to reach some sort of brink. Deep down knowing, your journey forward, is too far to turn back. As life seems to slip away, one last rolling number of times- is what you see. Crashing to shore. But within this break, there's no taking away. Instead, a cast- guiding you away. From what you left, into light. One last travel, sailing in flight.

Meandering:

Crickets to frogs, and the ways they chirp. Another drink, in prelude to a burp. Crawling and hopping, within scales or slime. All passing the day, making way through time. One sits in a chair, ears to ponder. As nature speaks, their language you wonder. Us all making sounds, chirps to a burp. I'll have my drink, to the bottom i'll slurp.

Lost in circles:

Lost in this wilderness. Ending my way back, to where I once stood. Filling these old footprints with new. Forever on the trek, of finding my way home. My vision forward, being blinded by invincible light. This journey forward, being covered by night. These sounds, forever being the same. Just to come back from where I came.

Moving on:

Just your sly shift to the left, brings me more to the right. Just your glance up, brings me more to gaze down. A slight zig in your step, breaks me to a zag. Your step forward, forces me to move back. What once was smooth as silk, now abrasive as sand. Your thoughts towards me, moving my thoughts away from you. What once was, shall never be. Your grasp around me, from now on, will never be.

So:

Set your hands so- towards the glass so. Make you feel ever so- slightly so. Reflection from the glass so- revelation from the past so- nostalgia feels so ever so. Turning away just so- the past behind just so- walking always slowly, as so.

Endless nights:

To think I should go to bed, what rings- are these thoughts that flow through my head. God sings, what I should live up to. But who's he, to tell me, who's who. Life temps, in the spring- what I do, and what it will bring. All I do, to drink, to further what's near. No longer to listen, to what I hear. So this dance, by myself- it's clear. What I live, to which I fear.

Hardened soft:

Tread lightly on this hardened soul, what seems so callous, is tender to touch, so heavy the ballast. Rough in the present, delicate to the past. These memories of hardship shall never pass. Tough and rugged, you see displayed. My mood in moment, so easily swayed. Before you speak, a thought in flight. Think of its pain, as teeth through a bite. As seen displayed, many times a disguise. A word of wisdom, a word to the wise. It's not always, as what it seems. Don't make the mistake, in thinking you know what it means. Leave it lie, in your moment of doubt. Their struggle their own, is a continuous bout.

Waiting for you:

So tired, so tired, on silky black sheets. This cold to ponder, as I cover my feet. Alone is my feel, gathering my thoughts. To lay here forever, covered with moss. Waiting for a knock, at my front door. To see your face, just once more. Pondering the day, which will never come. Reality sets in, to then be numb. Stoic and taut, I will forever wait. On silky black sheets, bearing the weight.

The Weeping Willow:

What such willow shall whip upon invisible tides of breeze. Lashing out, in such delicate whim. Reaching towards its highest of cascading limbs. To sway amongst a current, being blown through thousands of branches. Feeling as though you belong, within a soft blanket of nature's growth. The smell on your hands, after whistling down a long rope of leaves. In a way, having a kind of bond. One that never leaves, one, which will be there tomorrow. Casting shade over a hot day, or shielding, against cold, blistering winds. Traits that bare scarce among your own, but seem to blossom, under an old willow.

Warming to thaw:

Through stiffness of winter, with prevail of spring thaw. Birds once gone, now sing through a luke warm dusk. Low casting, fragmented clouds- reflect a warmer sun. Working out a winters rust. Loosens to a step, with a little more spruce. With winter, it's cloudy forecast of cold bringing a sense to appreciation for those times of warm. To days becoming longer, and temperatures becoming hotter- only a Midwesterner can know.

Finished from past:

Memories seep into regret. No one, not one, can linger through the past without an action, which if wished, you could take back. Regret, being tough like a callous. Looking down at your hands. Reminding one of the ware. What friction brought on such thick skin. Memories of which, create a sense of wisdom. Bringing on a method. When applied, able to avoid such action. One can only reach the light, by voyage through darkness. Sun shines on the grit. Grit accumulated through mistakes. The closest thing to perfection is imperfection, blemishes of our past. Being polished over time. Like a diamond being forged, under the pressures of turmoil. Being heated, hammered, bent and forged. We are all, eventually finished products, of what we once were.

Sounds:

The essence of sound, at times rings silent. It's that tone of silence. A faint ring of solitude, which reminds one of peace. Days shrinking to hours, as sound ripples. A tidal wave of noise, shrinking time. All one needs to hear, from time to time, is static noise- to hear nothing.

Living through life:

Crisp sounds dimmed through a distance of smog and mist. Tires and hustle coasting at some unforeseen rate. Standing still, as mind and drive travel beyond galaxies and plains. Working as hard as needed; creating like, shining upon foreseen future. Casting a gaze among obstacles routes. Taking the path, worn by few. Relishing in a future being traveled towards. Living in this mind of open fields; blooming thoughts of tomorrow, within today. Live within now, living for the future.

Flying together:

Wind sways me left, to the right. Beneath my wings, rolling in flight. Flying with fellows, with much purpose. Intentions so strong, being so earnest. Soaring near, it's rolling cloud. Bellows no fear, pronouncing out loud. Wing to wing, tip to tip. Brothers forever, clenching in grip. To a swoop, we shall glide. With every moment, taking with pride.

One who creep:

Who are you, the one who creep? Deep my slumber, mellow so deep. Creaks on old, worn-out floor. Seeking a thought, breaking the bore. Drowsy solemn, wakes to be curious. In hopes of intentions, not beyond serious. Asking in thought, realizing the hour. Firm in my tone, he crouches to cower. Discerning his fear, I mellow my voice. Calming to speak, inviting rejoice. Simple his words, asking in question. Lonely his eyes, a sad expression. All I need, is a brief assistance. To break my lows, relentless their persistence. In that moment, I remember the times. A companion being needed, receptive of the signs. A hand being lended, to one in need. To not be alone, the one to plead.

Spry motivation:

I might, as to seek revelation through clouded mind. Blistering through encapsulation, thoughts of what's ahead. Conjuring a spry sense of intense motivation to pronounce, and dignify my conviction. A rolling idea of reckoning sprouts through dignity. Throwing away its quality, for what needs to be heard. Shredding words, gashing through ears, seeming deaf to ones words. Bringing bouts of tribulation- an acute frustration. Turning to persistence, a relentless grind. A voice being heard, paying the price.

Within yourself:

Singing in prance, a tune no-one can hear. Light to shine, when surrounded by dark. Grazing tall fields of weed, without a soul being seen. Dancing in rhythm, within solo of yourself. Finding what's green, in pastures of rust. Marveled with intrigue, in solemn so bleak. Eyes lie on beauty, when seeming so ugly. Taking tidbits of life, left on the ground. Finding your peace, when there's none to be found.

Remembering Him:

Time comes to a moment, when one realizes it's gone, forever. A long, deep conversation. Stories in prelude- to laughs, cries, and life lessons. Wisdom being found, in a singular person. So many instances, seeming to last forever- in some impossible fashion. In that moment, the penetrating realization of time. It's unrelenting, always sustaining the ability to give and to always take away. Every grain, each and every speck that sprinkles the mosaic of our lives, eventually washes away. Being forced to adapt, in some impossible fashion. As if vulnerability strikes when you're most exposed. Feeling as if ready, only to realize you're not. In this passage of time, there being moments of loss. Most can be salvaged, reinvented, overcame, replaced- but others not. A loss of something that is gone forever. Never to speak, never to console. Our stories, laughs, cries- being gone. Never to be replaced. As if this departure is taking a piece from yourself. Life being as such- finicky in its ways. Right to left, seeming to zig and zag. If life had a twin, it would be time. Always understanding each-other- when nothing else does. Time explains the story of life. Ever changing, always fluid. Peaks crashing to a low level. So as I sit, holding the hand of a man, who influenced me like nothing else will. I speak alone, only to myself. Crying for a moment, just a moment- to have a chance to speak once more. Hearing his voice, once more. Hearing his stories, once more. One more instance of breath, once more. Knowing it won't come. As life always succumbs to time. It's ripple, always finding a shore. It's tide, always receding; but to never return. Feeling stranded, in search of a sail- and for a breeze to guild me away, from what I feel. If he could speak, one last time- I have a feeling of what he would say... "Remember me, as if in the light. How lucky we were, our journey in flight. Having the best, the greatest of times. Nothing we couldn't handle, our mountains we climbed. Our love being captured, in so many of moments. Our bond after death, to never be broken. Celebrate my life, when things were best. Remember me, in life we were blessed." Taking this thought to myself- I realize what I have. Family as a sail, friends as my breeze, blowing me away. Support I have, because of him. What I am, because of him.

Two Suns:

Two suns- to shine on both sides. One so warm, and the other so cold. Both sides you see. Accept me, both sides. So warm, and so cold. Ride with me- so fast, and so slow. Talk with me- so shallow, and so deep. Run with me, where to? Neither know. Jump with me- a leap of faith. Falling together- landing together. Worthy of me- worthy of you. Both seeing dark- on both sides. Both seeing light- on both sides. Take me for me, and I'll take you. Eachother together- sharing our two suns.

Threads of memories:

Threads to flicker against stiff breeze. Sounds level at a whistle, where the old clothes were left to hang. Seeming to be left for ages; as the shirts look of old rags, and jeans no longer resemble crisp. Those smells of old, dirty socks and stained overalls that mom would elbow; over soapy suds, and water cold from the well. My nose no longer turns to a flowery scent. These clothes are no longer clean. The line no longer tended. Only threads of memories, to flicker against stiff breeze.

Not to care what others think:

Take me a walk, outback alone. No one to judge, my presence unknown. Thoughts turn to talk, only to myself. Opinions of others, left to themselves. This seeming easier, than telling my fable. To ones who judge, branding a label. At least more than once, acting not yourself. These feelings I assume, just put to the shelf. One day in hopes, a feeling will come. That the thoughts of others, will grow to be numb.

Comforts of home:

A lonely boy, wandering to roam. Lost and scared, unable to find home. Fears of creatures, lurking in the night. Remembering the words, "It's going to be all right." Thoughts drifting back, being put to bed. Warm stories being told, from a book mom read. Her voice so soft, assuring not to fear. Those noises and creeks, he always hears. Tucking him in, and turning off the light. Mom says goodnight, no need to fright. Waking up, from this frightening dream. Almost to shout, bellowing with scream. Realizing the warmth, safe in his room. Almost as if, he's cradled in the womb. Returning back, to a calming sleep. Knowing he's safe, to count the sheep.

Courage:

A bloody sea, of crimson red. So many lay, maimed and dead. Bullets and bombs, create a static. In chaos so grim, a scene so traumatic. Brothers in arms, taking fire. Courage so great, one has to admire. Men and women, going to battle. Bravery is certain, unable to rattle. Coming home, after the fight. Having to adjust, hoping they might. Some find light, after the dark. Peace after war, wanting to embark. Visiting your comrades, who made it home. Either in person, or facing their stone. Embracing in hug, or with a prayer. Reminiscing experiences, only the few can share.

The spoils of the grind:

Unlucky for one, luck to another. A conundrum to ponder, a thought to wonder. Seeming so easy, for others you observe. Wanting the gift, convinced you deserve. Failing to realize, with the people who work. That fortune falls, with the ones who lurk. Through times of struggle, thick and thin. Having the will, crawling to win. Riches in life, only to be captured. By ones who fight, battered and tattered. Two kinds of people, exist in this life. The ones willing to work, and the others of strife. Before you scoff, at others and their fortune. Realize they gave, more than their portion.

Times in between:

It's four seasons, so they say. What about in between, in times of gray? Spring being wet, blossoms to sprout. Failed to be mentioned, before the clout. Or summer being warm, dried to a perk. Not seeming to capture, even a fake of a smirk. Fall being bright, blasting with color. Feeling so tight, choking through the collar. Winter to cold, in snow so festive. Not wanting to see, a soul not rested. To the four, mapped out seasons. Sometimes forgetting, the ones with the demons.

Not what it seemed:

Blistering bliss, at the speed of light. Not knowing that love, can reach such height. Meeting at first, no more than a stranger. Failing to see, any cause for danger. Seeming to say, everything so right. It's timing so perfect, from dark I see light. So long on this road, thoughts of forever I'd roam. Your warmth being captured, finding my way home. As time passes on, going with the flow. Your riddle I decipher, beginning to decode. Myself to settle, no one else to ponder. Your mind to drift, your eyes to wander. At once convinced, having it figured out. My thoughts to shift, this feeling of doubt. No longer knowing, where I stand. Our sands of love, falling though my hand. Our time being brief, left only to memory. Skin turning tough, calloused and leathery. Back on the road, lonely to trek. Picking up pieces, after the wreck. Time rolls on, its effect being magic. Now looking back, not seeming so tragic. Willing to hold out, for true love you reserve. Knowing yourself, and what you deserve. Taking each moment, in hard times of lesson. Learning that amity, takes time and progression.

Just to do it again:

Antsy with boredom, before light through blackness. Plotting a way, with lines on the atlas. Conjuring joke, breaking stagnant with laugher. Hoping that time, flies from thereafter. One turns to three, feeling like four. Getting through this night, seeming such a chore. Sitting to ponder, this dragging bore? Getting to that point, heading for the door. Finally through the drag, heading for home. Just to turn around, treading once more.

Not to care:

You care? I could care less. Not worth the bare, fuck the stress. Karen said what? I could give two shits. Shrugging it off, I have to admit. Word on the street, that gossip is heavy. Keep it coming, that shits so petty. You really wanna know, how I feel? No fucks to give, I fail to conceal. Next time you wander, in my direction. Save the bullshit, fuck your objection.

Moving on, as I cant:

Love me not- seeming to forget what we had. Time standing still in my world. As it seems to travel so fast in yours. I dwell in a past, seeming so far from where you are now. Why can't I forget? When you have no issues doing so. You want, what's best of both worlds for yourself. Wanting me to be ok with you, as you're ok with someone else. People work in ways, which contrast to what works for yourself. When you burn, it hurts and it leaves a mark. This mark on myself, which I didn't leave on you. All it takes, is a look to remind myself. This glance I speak, you cannot relate.

Three Birds:

Three birds below a lonesome cloud. Above something dead. Smells rising up, swooping to the ground. 9am light, brightest till noon. This time I look up. Three birds fly, alone in front of blue. Beneath a cloud, lonely in the sky.

Leaving solitude:

A lonely trek on the track towards solitude. A slight ring in the ear perks a sensation of remoteness. The one and only thing to listen to; restless noise between my head. A desolate bellow coming from an unforeseen distance telling me to come home. Home, being left, searching for new. The call back, no longer home. Waiting for a shriek through blinding darkness to lead the way. Asking for the guiding song to take me there. Seeking rhythm in every step. A dismal tread, turning to song and dance. Heavy strides, pivot to a ballroom dance. At last, a spiraling tune. Taking me towards, the glimpse of a new.

Relishing:

So many lives lost in the eyes of the living. Growing old, with so many falling short of elder ago. To reminisce with the young, of the old past. Only yourself to understand what you speak. The trip far west, remembered by only the ones who have passed. Bringing home a tune, sung by only the departed. Sulking in what once was... convincing the future of the greatness, of the gone.

Drunk and lonely:

You can stare at something forever, and always forget what it looks like. Those moments of smoke rolling off. Failing to capture the pattern. Vision narrows through a tunnel. Drunk in thoughts of nothing. To recall what you've seen, only to remember nothing. As a bee lands on your ear, with no reaction. So deep in yourself, in this moment so shallow. Feeling so sad, with a feeling of apathy. Another swig to wet what's dry, drying the tears so wet. Displacing yourself from emotion, finding yourself so alone. That smoke flicked, left to burn out. Just to light another. Hearing life in the distance, bringing me back home.

Before you hang:

Heavy hangs from rope, the weight to shred. Life without peace, taut to a dread. Stepping to stool, before you sway. Think of the light, brightness to day. Before giving life, dangling in sway. Drift back to peace, finding another way. Sometimes not found, in moments of dismay. So many of those, that would love you to stay. Don't fall to mistake, limp from a lynch. Remember that life, is a treasure to clench.

Our love, will forever blossom:

My love- something you never say until you have a reason to say it. It's like the words I love you. Not spoken until you feel it so intensely with another person. Or making a promise to do anything for that individual- to literally give everything you have in sacrifice for another. Having feelings so deep and intense, one cannot fathom logic to translate into words. In life you sometimes stumble onto magic; which cannot be described in either sonnet, nor a tune. Only being able to express through feelings and actions. Sometimes in tear, or through touch. This magic I speak is the infinity of love, commitment, and for the journey. Compassion you can smell. Your companion you can see. Their body you can touch. A voice you can hear. And the spices of life you can taste. Knowing after a long day, your partner has your back. They're in your corner. Willing to fight, scrap, claw and tear. Only in love, can you find everything good in this world within one. To my love. To my life. To our life. To forever be one. Amongst this planet, and throughout the cosmos. In the sprout of spring, or within the stars. Our love, our life, will forever blossom.

9/11:

Nine eleven, we all remember. Emotions so strong, unable to measure. Knowing that moment, your place in time. Three thousand to perish, the ultimate crime. Planes take to flight, towards destination. Taken my terror, a sick act of demonstration. Without hesitation, first to respond. Heroes were born, a nation to bond. At once divided, together we now stand. From that day forward, embracing in hand. Remember lives lost, and the families to grieve. Showing them our support, through prayer we weave. Only here, our nation so great. Able to fight back, only we can create. Eighteen years, seeming so long. Forever we stand, a country so strong.

Suicide:

I heard it in the wind, a voice to make me cry. So bleak and grim. The thoughts of suicide. Bleeding out, my body dried. To contemplate, the thoughts of suicide. A voice of drive, the hand to guide. Steering me away, from thoughts of suicide. Heavy this ponder, brain to fry. So real the mistake. The thoughts of suicide. Fighting the dark, with feelings of pride. Taking me away, from thoughts of suicide. Driving fast, to home I ride. Unable to care, the thoughts of suicide. To hits that come, taking in stride. Dodging what drives, these thoughts of suicide. So many fought, countless have tried. Resisting the urge, thoughts of suicide. Many who care, advice in stride. Unable to relate, to thoughts of suicide. Unstoppable meeting immovable, forces collide. Unable to move, these thoughts of suicide. Irrational to most, emotion to misguide. Spiraling down, thoughts of suicide. Bounded by strain, in hopes to unbind. Breaking through conviction, thoughts of suicide. Asking how I feel, in reply I lie. Masking of guilt, these thoughts of suicide. Wanting for truth, this notion to subside. Hanging by a rope, thoughts of suicide. Wanting to be happy, requests have been denied. Rolling down the cliff, towards thoughts of suicide. Towards the brink of forever, this moment I decide. Unable to handle, these thoughts of suicide. Ones who are happy, conflicting feelings that divide. Between you and I, these thoughts of suicide.

Finding Faith:

Looking up, to rain pouring down. Resuming my stare, I assume to drown. Pour mixed with tear, concocting a potion. Toxic it spills, down my face with emotion. Screams without sound, no echo with silence. Pleading for help, a voice of guidance. This belief I seek, nowhere to be found. Standing so soaked, my feet to the ground. Now more than ever, desperate in search. To bath my feet, for god in his church. Faith the gift, I have yet to receive. In times of doubt, alone to grieve. My palms to press, towards the sky. For view of reason, prayers seemed denied. In final attempt, closing my eyes. Fighting the urge, of credence to die. Blinded by white, what seems to be light. Leaving this earth, taking to flight. Landing on steps, at the gates of heaven. Alone with god, to bare my confession. "I live with mistakes, my lessons learned. Forgiveness from you, I hope to have earned." Time comes to one, singular moment. To hear god speak, his wisdom heard spoken. "Love for you, was never lost. The life you live, is paying the cost." "The faults one makes, backing the debt. By learning from mistakes. Your reasons for being wet." "Standing in rain, asking for advice. Seeking gods faith, is funding the price." "Your place in my grace, after life finding peace. This worry you bear, I grant you release." Casting me down, back to the ground. Faith so certain, at last to be found.

Dark:

Unfortunate you came, on such a dark day. A mood so grim, falling to the gray. A stride not stepped, with best foot forward. Peaking with rage, sanity crossing the border. Ambivalent not, my voice to crack. Showing myself, a side so black. Madness surreal, best left alone. Not wanting to reveal, this dark side to be known. To any given day, seeming so relaxed. Catching my streak, bleak and detached. At times unable, to keep temper to an idle. Digressing back, unleashing my primal.

Thoughts to a stranger:

One last drink, to a final smoke. To tell you how much, my soul is broke. Spilling out troubles, of the common folk. To a total stranger, onto ears of a bloke. I don't expect, for you to remember. That faithful night, the dark of December. The dreaded moment, month twelve, day eight. Searching for peace, to find my faith. Another go, thirty times come around. The faith I seek, nowhere to be found. In hope of next, to come thirty-one. My mind to rest, the search to be done. From day one to the present. Always in search, to bath my feet, for god in church. Faith the gift, I have yet to receive. In times of doubt, alone to grieve. Time comes to one, singular moment. To hear god speak, his wisdom heard spoken. "In time of struggle, no need to be wise. I'm here with a shoulder, soaking your cries."

Drifting tides of love:

Tide, to push us away. Love, will always remain. Scared, of needing you. Afraid, you seeking new. Sunny, so dark and tan. Romance, we can draw freehand. Excitement, our special brand. Always, being unplanned. Grains, lust in sand. Gripping, a rush so grand. Time, being so brief. Desire, turning over a new leaf. Wanting, room to grow. Passion, now dim from a glow. Leaving, our private beach. Outstretched, beyond my reach. Left, only with memory. Craving, our bond of energy.

The rhythm of life:

The rhythm of life, a long road to travel. Hitching a ride, mounted on the saddle. This journey going smooth, soon veers to gravel. Times becoming tough, clenching to straddle. Peaks roll to valleys, from lows to ascend. Realizing the turns, having so many bends. From cities to fields, buildings to grass. As time treks on, scenery will pass. From light to dark, sun becomes moon. From black of night, rising to noon. Youthful appearance, turns to a crinkle. Bloom to frayed, ending in a wrinkle. Cold raises to hot, breaking out in sweat. Drought tears to rain, thirsty to wet. Heavy is life, unable to bear the weight. Wanting to give up, many can relate. To many of those, willing to wait. Happiness can grow, success to await. Existing through a ripple, a moment in time. Deep in a hole, your moment to climb. Gripping to handle, learning to sway. Figuring out, finding your way. From start to end, learning from the road. Joy being captured, the riddle you decode. Caper with swing, to the rhythm of life. Once seeming wrong, proves to be right.

The Softened Beast:

Gazing sight on the beast, tearing through the flesh. Feasting on the carcass, that is ever so fresh. It looks up to see, myself being frightened. His senses to turn, his conscious becomes heightened. What seems to be vicious, lacking the care. A creature that kills, not wanting to scare. Instinct so innate, unable to control. The outpour of rage, I witness unroll. His eyes become soft, not wanting to see. The judgment in me, that I want to plea. The beast turns to speak, to my upmost surprise. This shock of a tear, he starts to cry. Explaining his trek, through the hardships of survival. I realize my way, doesn't stand to rival. Myself being tame, not knowing the means. Of having to eat, what you're forced to slay. I start with response, in mind of his empathy. Towards the things he kills, my words of sympathy. Not knowing the way, of having to be savage. What the beast wants most, is understanding to be salvaged. Behind the fur, the teeth and the muscle. Lies a soft heart of guilt, hidden in the shuffle. Thinking yourself as noble, advanced in evolution. Our lives that we live, are just in delusion. A beast such as this, brutal in his protrusion. Should remind ourselves, of how much we are unproven.

Sailing on:

Pounded by storm, saturated with doubt. Beginning to ponder, this feeling of clout. Looking back through time, changing the past. Smoldering in my mind, this gloomy forecast. Seeking for change. I look towards the bow. Starting from stern, I wonder the how. Breaking through tide, plunging through waves. This one thing I know, is what everyone craves. The salvation of peace, keeping in mind. The journey onward, is leaving regrets behind.

Aged Wisdom:

Look to a face, of ripened old age. So many of the elder, glare to the youth with rage. The calloused hands of a long life of work. Compared to the softness, of the boys that chirp. Men talking the talk and backing it up. To this generation, still drinking their milk from a cup. A strong, aged mind sifting through the shit. These younger folk, not knowing the meaning of true grit. To claw and grind, through the thick and thin. The old teaching the young, what it takes to win.

Rejuvenating harmony:

Only in dream, this shift in symphony of verse. Sounds being played, so widely diverse. Dancing like birds, prancing in sleep. It's toll to resonate, my slumber so deep. What keeps me awake, no longer at play. I assume to rest, snoozing through the day. Brightness of sun, casting a shadow. Unable to penetrate, this doze for fallow. Restored with rest, fertile and awake. From dawn until dusk, challenges I can take. From invention and fantasy, proving so real. Good for the soul, it's impact I feel. Grooving to harmony, behind closed eyes. Proving that dreams, can never die.

Women of the wise:

As filter fades, he admits to being drunk. Undoubtedly the portray, convinced he's a hunk. Laying it down, assured of his confidence. Showing with pride, this feeling of competence. You peel back the disguise, exposing his layer. A weak hearted fool, the game of a player. To let it roll out, his act to attract. Almost to be fooled, in knowing you retract. Standing so stout, his ego to wait. Like hook to a fish, hoping you take the bait. Playing along, like he's so great. Knowing without doubt, you're no cheap date. Being so wise, to a man's deceit. Having this boy beat, he could never compete. Returning the favor, laying it down. After you're done, making him feel like a clown. Advice from a man, before you get blitzed. Know when you're tanked, opportunities will be missed. Playing a game, with the class of a woman. Shutting you down, realizing you couldn't.

Crooked Ol' Pete:

Crooked ol' Pete, walked with a limp. So many to ponder, where he got his gimp. The legend of Pete, never to lie. A tall tale told, he could never die. Riding white lightening, into the city. Started this story, of a life so gritty. The beginning of resistance, into prohibition. Pete fought back, with a relentless mission. Never for glory, of reaching the pinnacle. His reasons were sound, based upon principle. "Don't take from me, making trouble. Leave me to be, this hick behind the stubble." "See your way out, back to Chicago. I'll do as I please, transporting my cargo." So goes the accounts, of this history so sweet. Of the ones who scrapped, with the fierce ol' Pete. Cracking his stills, with the blade of an ax. Pete stands firm, "I won't pay your corrupt tax." Hostility grows, bullets fly. Taking a few, ol' Pete you can't buy. Prying out, from flesh the lead. Crooked ol' Pete, still left undead. Behind the cheroot, a face seeking revenge. Willing to die, for drink he defends. Cutting off, a toe for a trinket. Letting all know, ol' pete has no limit. Making a stand, against odds so great. Etched into stone, to prevail is Pete's fate. Fighting through, making the climb. Pete stands true, through the test of time. So as you drink, a cold sip of booze. Thank crooked ol' Pete, having the guts to refuse.

Together:

Would you lay down for me? I'd lay down for you. Willing to do, for so very few. When that moment comes, in time of struggle. No need for doubt, I'll lay down the knuckle. Finding no choice, but to grapple on the mat. Not far behind, ready to go to bat. Someone willing, to give you a slap. Always know, I'll have your back. Nothing too black, when things turn dark. You and I, will leave a mark. As many as ten, to face us two. With each others help, we'll see it through. Spilling our blood, in the same mud. Doing it together, you'll always be my bud. Knocking us down, we'll give it a "yup". Helping each other, we grip to get up. So just remember, when times are tough. I'm there by your side, when the going gets rough.

Nashville:

The city of dreams, the ones with a voice. Where so many have fun, with music we rejoice. This town of hope, few to make a name. My place in Nashville, for friends and family I came. Waiting in line, in the rain we pray. To catch that tune, we've longed to hear play. From old George Straight, to the rhythm of Kid rock. These melodies we crave, keep rolling without stop. Bumming a smoke from a stranger, dancing with a lady. The night being young, partying like crazy. The stomp of boots, rocking on the floor. This song and dance, vibrating to my core. Bars closing down, through the crowds I shiver. To end my night, by the Cumberland River. Relative in blood, or a friend from the past. With the ones I love, these memories will last. At last we proclaim, not to be bashful. Let it all out, in the city of Nashville.

Persistence:

Attention to your gallop, that beautiful stride. Pardon my stare, I can't seem to hide. Running from which, you seek temptation. My urge to slip, my attempt at flirtation. Your speed to increase, as I pursue the chase. A surge to outrun, my ambition you cannot outpace. Stamina to a peak, breathing becomes heavy. In hopes to catch up, I stand at the ready. You start to slow down, at last I embrace. Finally within, sharing your space. To witness up close, eager in waiting. Your response as to why, my presence you're evading. With reply you admit, your reluctance to commitment. My advances towards you, are met with resistance. I ask why, my feelings so strong. This devotion to you, wanting for so long. All I ask, is to give me a chance. To show you that life, can be lived in romance. To my surprise, your reverse in direction. Willing to give, your zeal of affection.

Living for you:

Shoes left unfilled, your legacy so great. Me having to step in, unable to bear the weight. The influence you had on so many lives. Doubting my ability to have your formidable drive. Lending a hand to so many of those. Impacting the lives, of the people you chose. This burden to honor heavy on my chest. Questioning my potential to carry on your quest. Maintaining pursuit of what you did best. Inspiring others, this gift you were blessed. To uphold your distinction, I will stand the test. The least I could give, is my life to invest.

Infidelity:

Traveling long distance, what seems to be hours. To smell your scent, the aroma of flowers. The destination near, dodging slow traffic. Blazing towards home, what follows so tragic. What I love most, lying in bed. Under the blankets, is what every man dreads. Yelling to proclaim, making the mistake. Subsiding to urge, your decision I can't shake. My heart torn out, ripping through my chest. By the one I adore most, I never would've guessed. Asking to forgive, your tone so stressed. I propose the suggestion, for you to get dressed. What comes next? How to react rationally? In the midst of your act, your display of infidelity. Conjuring up, the words to conceive. Telling you firmly, it's best if you leave. Destroying our intimacy, asking to come back. My sympathy for you, I'm seeming to lack. As you walk out, knowing it's the end. A second chance granted, I'm unwilling to lend.

Snow:

Once upon a time, not too long ago. Ever so adventurous, playing in the snow. Waiting for that moment, to roam with the ones you know. Ever so youthful, playing in the snow. With blistering cheeks, and a runny nose. Not thinking of tomorrow, playing in the snow. As youth turns to age, beginning to grow. Becoming so mature, beginning to dread the snow. What used to be fun, making snowballs to throw, at your childish friends, making memories in the snow. Life being serious, having to show. Demeanor so serious, longing for the snow. Taking a glimpse back, to the times that glow. Ever so happy, in your time in the snow

The giver:

A whisper in your ear, my intimate secrets. These thoughts I carry, heavy in their bleakness. You seem to convey, a certain wisdom. Trying to pry out, the insight from your prism. So transparent and giving, willing to extend. The advice much needed, helping a friend. Your insight so great, unable to repay. Wishing I could, finding a way. Insisting I relax, counsel is free. Peace of mind I give, putting your mind at ease.

Violated:

Exposing myself, to show you what's left. Letting you in, as an exclusive guest. Lying on cold, what seems to be concrete. You play me, like a fading downbeat. Striding over, like i'm a laid down jacket. Keeping your feet dry, while ignoring my racket. Packing me down, into the ground. Subsiding my ability, to ever make a sound. As I get up, from an experience so degrading. Realizing that instant, you entering was invading. Casting you out, this moment is done. No longer allowing, your moment of fun.

Not always what it seems:

Looking in through the window. What seems so close from a distance, is so very far apart up close. The disguise of stability as to not rock the boat. What it seems to others, living beyond your wildest dreams. From within, existing only to maintain the peace. What you deem figured out, is far from correct. What looks so obvious, is usually never that direct. To point a finger, as to pinpoint the truth. Seeming to forget, you're not in the loop. Looking through the window, what seems so close from a distance. Is so very far apart, when up close to their existence. What it looks like to others, living beyond your wildest dreams. Not knowing the reality, that nothing is what it seems. Stepping outside, to put on a show. Hoping that no one catches on to what you know. In a glimmer of aspiration, to turn what's fake into reality. Hoping that someday, your ambition becomes normality.

Normandy:

Normandy, a day to remember. Raising the flag, a moment to recall. Ones who fought, died, came home as one; or leaving a piece behind. Keeping in mind freedoms granted; knowing the cost of a drop of blood, or a restless mind after the war fought. Place your respect where it's due. On this day, straying towards the ones you know- but keeping in mind the ones you don't. The uniform, the brave, the men and women giving what's necessary. On this day, take a moment and pray. Regardless of lines in the sand; this one thing that needs to withstand. For the ones who gave the strain, to give us what we have today.

Can no longer give:

Ouch, to the prick of my finger. Why must you do this to me? Why, it's for you. As it drips, to think the worth of pain, and what you say is good for me. Another poke, to a prod, I nudge. Why must you do this to me? Why, it's for you. As it aches, to contemplate the worth of discomfort, and what you say is good for me. One last attempt, to do what is good for me, I draw back. What you find worthy for me, I cannot agree. What you want from me, I can no longer give. To prick, to prod, to poke, is no longer for me.

Broadened perspective:

To each their own, said the one willing to give a chance to another; with a slight different mindset of their own. The broad mind gives way to open thought. Makes one think of culture never being predicated on a narrow mind. The spectrum is broad, when willing to hear a voice other than your own. Intelligence is learned, by the willing. So much more is left unsaid by the reluctant. Times are stagnant upon resistant ears. Wiser than most proclaimed the melting pot is how we achieve. No wall stands between two of a different kind. Two as one they say, two as one.

Not that into me:

As to love, the signs and symptoms of a broken heart. Beating to a rate surpassing your own. The powerful force of romance struck down by the unwilling. Seeking satisfaction where it isn't granted. This feeling of unstoppable force meeting an infinite potency of resistance. Feelings opposite to my own. The emotion of willingness to give everything, circling the drain of unwillingness. My strive towards yours, with the back pedal of your own. A relentless speed losing ground towards your interminable streak. Falling short of your beginning.

Motions:

Motions, are you sick of the weather? This cascading fall of metaphoric emotion affects you and I. They say two minds are better than one... neither you, nor I, can figure it out. What's simple, plain to see, is definitely harder than ever to accomplish. What needs to be done, seems impossible. Until that day, when the forecast turns to light. Not so convenient for you, becomes a light in the sky for myself. As I turn to past, your feelings remain in the past. What's done is done- I render our done.

The odd and bizarre:

What lies beneath the wide smile of a seemingly habitual appearance, is a churning rage, casted behind a dark clout. One keeps at bay the urge to spill hidden feelings of twist and the unusual. The masked devil with fiery horns, cloaked under the dread of fitting within the norm. With scorching steam, and a clenched jaw, making way, through the day. The way to consolation, an expulsion of pressure for relief. Only so very few can relate. Let it be, the night for bizarre. Unsheathe the odd, and the strange, to release the extraordinary.

The demented:

Casting gaze into a glazed stare. Looking into a state of a confused mind. Unable to ask questions. Lacking the ability to expound on the day, or a blissful past. Lost in an amnesia of long lost time. Words spoken, strung together in to no particular order. Inept to make sense of the verbalization of thoughts. Starting in no specific place, ending up in an unknown realm. Everything ends up being random, with no significant meaning. A diminished mind is best left alone. Never to try making sense of it all. Avoiding attempts of re-orientation. Just to leave them living in their state of bewilderment. In hopes they find comfort in their solitude.

Rising above:

Dancing in this world of chaos. As if deficient of sight and sound. Our moment together shall not be diminished by what surrounds us. In a tight clench, allowing nothing to come between. Standing upright, as everything falls. Over the screams and cries, I hear her voice whispering into my open ear. The soothing sounds of assurance places me at ease. Feeling as if the ground were to crumble, we would float amongst the air, weightless in the heavy atmosphere. Maintaining this non-reactivity to the realness of our surroundings. Resting into each other. Bearing a shared weight. Weathering the storm in the shelter of one another.

Treading in the sea of blues:

Treading in the sea of blues. So harsh and relentless on the body. Colors of bruise manifest in the subdermal layers. Barely keeping life above a choppy surface, which sustains a residual warmth. Below the knees the chilly pressure of depth. Feeling the distinct separation between the two contrasting layers. I grip onto the thin glimmer of hope, fighting for prolonged life. On the fringe of forever abyss; I feel the helping hand of an outstretched arm. Holding on with whatever left. Able to hold on just long enough for renewed life. Being given a second chance, to never stray into the deep again.

Back and forth:

Artificial light, glowing the fog of night. Making my way towards a relentless grind. In hopes of what I am doing now, prevails to a better future. Currently finding myself in a perpetual gloomy forecast. Amidst this thought, my destination becomes near. My feelings are constant with this place. Falling short of a fulfilling venture. Such a long distance to travel for something so dreadful. Walking in, only to look forward to walking out. Unable to even fake a positive vibe. Telling myself this isn't me. Over time, I worry it will become my new identity. As negative as what surrounds me. Any kind of interaction becomes abrasive. A need for change flows though me with urgency. Looking forward to leaving for home, only to then have to return again.

The warmth of memories past:

Take me back to that place. Where so many of those loving memories were left behind. Hoping the gust of time hasn't carried them away. It's been so long ago. That place so far behind. What is left, a foggy, fragmented memory. Wanting to re-trace my steps from the present, back into the light of the past. This place so warm, so rich. Realizing I can only reminisce. Only able to feel a distant, radiating warmth from a past lost in the distance traveled.

Betrayal:

Oh, how you have changed. Once embracing an unwavering sense of nobility. Now, in the wake of breakdown, sitting back to witness the destruction of everything which mattered. Your un-relenting stare; blank as to no emotion, which was taken from you when the decision was made to give it all away. What has been lost can never be retrieved. Letting this coldness enter into our lives. You ending on the side opposite to ours. We express concern, fear; only to have our words fall on your ear as to only hear, and never to listen. I assume these heavy thoughts onto conversations to myself. Not able to articulate these feelings to others. The one who understands the most, incapable of carrying this weight; as to bearing the same clout as I, dealing with it in our own ways. Hoping time finds a way to alleviate.

Casual interactions:

Talk to me about anything. The sky, tomorrow, today. Not everything between you and I needs to be in depth. Our very best of times have been spent in the shallows of our experiences. Skimming what's on the surface, sharing between each other. We find ourselves at the end of a long, uneventful day. Let's try not digging for conversation; leaving it to an effortless pluck from a shifty display of meaningless events. Tossing them to the dais for our easy chatter. Leaving the mind to rest for now. So, let's be simple on an evening such as this. In no way warranting our toil.

A different point of view:

Restless, as to the thoughts permeating the mind. Seeking ventilation to relieve the pressure. A step outside yourself opens to a new outlook. Observing this advanced panorama; in hopes to arrange these mind-bending cogitations. Spilling your reflections of thought outward. Beginning to develop a new frame of reference, as to what was troubling. Turning your slant inward. Revelations start to fall into place, and finally develop a comfortable place to dwell within. Remembering this for the next time. When what seems so unsettled, can be rectified into clarity.

Forever within instability:

Never seeming to catch you within stability. Your wavering mood; like a vessel without destination on a changing sea. Myself being on board for too long. A sense of motion sickness, rolling with your swings. My attempts to center your emotions prove pointless. Catching you on a good day may very well end in a bad one. For me, your closeness is comforting. Reaching out my hand to yours; hoping to spread that feeling. My effort is met with retraction. As if my presence isn't desired. I begin to question what we have. What can make this worth the effort? How long will this last? Something so changing and undesirable shouldn't persist this long. That first love is so hard to shake. Always covering the bad with excuses. Waiting for a change. One may come, and usually does; but never seems to be lasting. Almost as if the false hope is purposeful. Does it come from her? Or the condition? Then I wake to an epiphany. An unwavering desire to end this torturous romance. No question as to what needs to be done. Following through, I feel the weight lift from myself. Anxiety let off like an exhale. Walking away, knowing I will never go back.

Riding it out together:

With you on this venture. Being told of its vast distance. To only seem so brief alongside you. Bending the winding ways, blazing through the trees. Taking the long road, so straight to the end. Only with you, our destination is the occasion. Seemingly pointless to plan out, as to anything being worth the time. Sharing that time together. Going with the natural flow. Not a care can be conjured. Looking forward to what's ahead. Knowing my feelings for you match those of yours towards me. Residing anywhere, either temporary or permanent. Glances towards one another. Comfortable in all dwellings. As to all this, the rest of my story will be played out with you. Two main characters in a long, fruitful course. Picking up those overseen pieces along the way. My ending will be rich; in hopes of yours concluding the same, with me.

Sitting by the fire:

My lower half warmed by a crackling fire. The flames go from a blue to a yellowish red, as they weave through the charred lumber stacked. Flames turn into a heated popping; spraying into the air tiny sparkling bursts; as to the fire's afterthought. Following them to the sky above me. Blending in with the stars. Shining through holes in the lightless back of night. Paying attention to a stiff wind breathing through a dense forest. Taking in a crisp inhale. Pausing before a slow release back into the brisk air. A comfortable feeling of hot and cold, mixed to a blend of luke-warm, which covers my body. No one around, as it needs to be. Thinking of sleep, only after a little more time. Letting this night float me away, then take me back. Ending on a fulfilled note. In hopes it won't be the last.

Together here, and far:

I entered your world as you were entering mine. Sunlight grazes my face with sensual warmth. Illuminating in the light of you. Unable to take a step back. Blazing forward to that hopeful future. Side by side, we travel the galaxies and stars; never in hopes of an ending horizon. Our minds on a perpetual journey. These bright colors of you and I, splashed on beautiful canvas. The flowers never die. No need for return; as to them never leaving. As we know, home is the final destination. Where we want us to go. Living out the end of days still relishing in the enduring warmth of our past together. At the end of our final day, we shall travel again. Through the galaxies and stars. Finding our new home in eternity.

Waking to a new day:

Darkness is frayed by the sprouting of light. The black shade gives way to blue. Morning awakens into life. Sleepy tones change to chirpy tunes. Natures living creatures come to life. Stretching out the nightly stiff. Coming to sense as the orange glaze of day gets everything ready for what's ahead. Stepping out into the crisp air. Joining the wakefulness of everyone else. Coming together, while being apart. We all shall enjoy this fresh start, under the sunshine.

Coming to terms:

Coming to terms with your feelings was beyond difficult. So contrast as to my own. Spending countless time thinking of what could be. Living within my mind this fantasy. What never existed, seeming so real. As though I could touch and feel the textiles of you and I. All this happening too soon, without reason. Never thinking to ask how you felt before playing into this elaborate figment of my imagination. I've grown to respect your lack of reciprocation of my feelings. Time, the ultimate closure. Its unwavering ability to heal, has placed comfort in me to move on. One day, I hope to play out the life I had planned for you and I.

A lonely, unfamiliar place:

Existing in an unfamiliar place. The prolonged passing of time diminishes youth, and prevails to age. Once a life of riches, shadowed by the reality of dependence. Privileges once granted so easily, now are lost. Wishing for loss of memory of the past, in hopes of comfort in the present, in this existence, in an unfamiliar place. Such a lonely, unfamiliar place.

I see, a seed to plant:

I see, a seed to plant. Giving love, in hopes of blossom. Sharing time as one. Giving as much as we receive. Growing together so close, in hopes of never ending apart. Taking in the light, and the earth. Sharing what is neither yours, nor mine. A mutual bond, always stronger together, and never apart. Eventually giving way to wilt. Our colors showing the results of long life. Our leaves fall, and spread along the ground. Leaving behind everything. In hopes of one to see, a seed to plant.

Anxiety:

The mind strains. My worry displaced out of reality. Backtracking, searching for the source of this anxiety. Once found, pulling it apart. Pealing back the layers. Painfully analyzing every facet. Picking through every piece. Somewhere inside, I realize the absurdity, which fights the other side; the side putting me through this. This relentless process of infinity. Starting from where I do not want to be, traveling through this headache, and ending at the beginning. My thoughts traveling at the speed of light. Unable to escape the gravity of this black hole, tearing away at my mind. The desire for light slips into the event horizon, turning to darkness. The physics of this condition forever sealed by the science of its reality. My mental state written out like an equation, already solved. Its calculation made up of perpetual worry. Its answer being tension. Left only in hopes of a breakthrough, setting me free.

Needing you:

Sustaining life, feeding off your energy. The presence of you, turning my flower to blossom. Every day, waking to the first day of spring. Not to fear a blistering cold day the next. Yourself, so naive, as to your influence, making me more intrigued. Seeming so effortless and natural. Almost as if by accident. Forcing me into an unstoppable urge to learn more. Pointless to resist. The everlasting light shines through you, casting no shadow. Illuminating my darkness. Somehow, looking for a way to bring you closer. My life becoming a part of yours. Times together, ending in your departure. Leaving a warm, remaining presence. Unaware of the feelings having a possible mutuality. Mustering uncharted courage. Bringing my feelings to the forefront. Things wanted most, never seeming easy to obtain. Physically so close, feeling as if I stand on the opposite end of an endless longitude. Maybe, one day, our gravities will collide. Our meaning in life having a common purpose; as to each other, needing one another.

The best kept secrets are within yourself:

Truth and lie is known by one, but not the other. Telling a secret in hopes it remains sacred does not ring true. Coming back around, to fall on your ears. You keep from me what isn't yours to have. Displaying your disgruntled demeanor, as to what you have heard. You dangle this secret in hopes I reach. Asking questions for answers; answers to which I should know. Not offering a chance to separate truth from fiction. You leave me with my anxiety, as to always wonder what you've heard. Finding myself defenseless in the ability to rectify the clarity. At the end of it, I do realize I've brought this onto myself. Those best kept secrets are the ones you maintain within. Forever locked away. Protected from those who dwell on the spread of others fragile pieces of themselves.

The Voyager:

The burning fire of curiosity fuels the desire for adventure within the voyager. Starting from what is known, to venture into, and through the unknown. Their unwavering crave for discovery leads down a path of uncertainty, and shadows the thoughts and feelings of fear. Keeping in mind of what they have left behind. The security and comfort of home never filled the void within. The urge to start something new. To build a legacy on their own foundations. Not predicated on others. Living and breathing the freedom of self-exploration. Learning in ways never possible in the life lagging behind. Not knowing what lies beyond the visible gaze is the motivation that keeps the voyager on track; moving forward towards fulfillment. Living by rules set upon your own beliefs. This voyager never sleeps, never waivers in the resistance of what may lurk ahead. The voyager climbs, swims, walks, and keeps the chin beyond the chest; always in search for something new and unexploited, waiting to be touched. The voyager lives within us all. Waiting to be tapped into. Taking the leap of faith, into the unknown, is the start to a journey towards yourself.

Calling me home:

I stand at the foot of an immense grassy field. Casting my gaze upon the distance, I see a tall line of willows, just blocking the sprouting sun breaking through the horizon. The song of birds in the distance warming this feeling of calm; which radiates through my extremities. As if their whistling tunes were meant for me. I step into the tall grass with an outstretched hand. Feeling it graze below my palm. This place keeps all my senses hard at work. Waiting to awake from this dream, so it seems to be. Trying to store into memory this place, as to knowing I will have to leave soon. My blissful state is soon broken by a faint voice in the distance; telling me to come home. Forcing myself to turn around, I leave such beauty and solitude behind me; hoping to return. As to now, when the day seems long, and my patience wears thin; I look back on that day. Slowly shuffling through those memories carefully stored. As if I was there again.

Surrounded by lonely nothing:

Existing, feeling the weight of so much commotion. Surrounded by what seems everything, but feeling so alone. Unable to relate to anything meaningful. The obligation to interact, only conflicts with your desire for privacy. Being human is the desire for social interaction. This lack of desire calls into question your sanity. Are you losing what is meant to fill an individual? What makes us unique? Left only with a shell of what you once were. Becoming so fragile to life. Having to navigate this existence ever so carefully, as not to break what little is left. The only thing between functionality and destruction is a thin veneer; disguising what is left beneath. The intense pressures of your surroundings threatens what you're trying to preserve. Knowing eventually, this could crush you into something unrecognizable. Unable to repair, no chance for recovery. From then forward, forever drifting aimlessly towards a meaningless end.

Deaths Gates:

Walking through deaths gates. Living and breathing. My feet trek the path worn by the departure of life. Channeling my thoughts to imagine these lives once lived. Now buried in the ground. Each individual beginning, unrelated, never crossing paths. Now lie side-by-side. So briefly living apart, and now laid to rest next to one another for eternity. I approach a stone. So worn with age. Forgotten, so far removed from the present. The memory has died of this once alive soul. His meaning in life eroded to a fine dust, never to be noticed again. This man's ripple in time has reached the shore long ago. As my shadow casts over his resting place, I pay tribute to a stranger. His early time, etched into stone, reminds me of deaths unpredictability. Its unwavering nature to end what lives. Knowing that in time, I will soon enter deaths gates. No longer able to contemplate a life once lived. Time will erode my stone, into a fine dust. My ripple in time will find a shore, and the memories I left for others will eventually fade away.

Wanting to embrace again:

I find myself in a bedbound state. Living with age I never presumed to reach. Taking more than a few moments to orientate back to present. Your return, from your prolonged stay. We embrace, as though separating will never have a second chance. Beginning our romance in promising times. Swaying to the dance of a good life. What was dreamed became reality. Our lows prevailed to highs. Giving so much to each other. Never taking too much from one another. Dying tomorrow will end a fulfilled destiny. With no real regrets to ponder. Your time falling short of mine. One thing I always feared. So I wake from this reflecting dream.

Learning within the wasting of time:

You know where I am. That designated spot we both agreed upon. So much was built up to this point. So many questions prepared for this time. Meeting for that first time. Materializing my creation of you in my head. Ready for you to prove me right about you. Excuses eventually stretch thin to transparency; able to see through to the truth. Looking back, would you have been honest with your intentions? Wasting my time only in turn wastes your own. You are proof, relinquishing the fact as to what I am looking for, being so elusive, incredibly hard to find. I will digress back to square one. The silver lining is to what I have learned from you. Learning more from you with never meeting. Based on the assumption I would have learned nothing from meeting you.

Day to day:

As day turns into night, the sun no longer casts the shadows as the moon takes over. The sounds of light are taken over by the static of darkness. The ability to see for miles gives way to the inability to cast gaze. As some take pleasure in the warmth of noon, others seek shelter in the brisk of midnight. The sun rises, skirts along the sky, and sets into the horizon. All on the clock of relentless time. As I look along an endless plain, gazing at the fading sunset, thinking back on the day, I then steer my thoughts towards the next day. As day turns into night, night will prevail to day.

A childhood dream:

In bed, within a room only lit by the moon, it outlines the window. As I stare, the window appears much closer than it really is. My mind drifts back to a memory of the old house. On the floor, staring out the window with my family in the room. I was floating within the void of being awake and falling asleep. Staring at the window, it appeared much closer than it really was.

A walk towards clarity:

Walking down the road on a dark, brisk night. Looking up, breathing in the cool air. My eyes squint from the crisp sensation in my nose. There are more stars out tonight than there were the night before. The chill takes away any smell. The stones beneath my feet displace my steps. The dim light of the night outlines the structures of the landscape. Then comes a breeze that rolls through my hair. The sounds are everywhere; putting my thoughts and emotions at ease. At that moment, I remember moments of my life. Of being happy, free, full of emotion. The thought creates goosebumps all over my body. The breeze is now behind me, with hands in my pockets. At this point, I could walk forever. Alone with my thoughts. Hashing out the day, figuring out problems, coming to conclusions. Everything is on the table. Where I'm at, on the road, in the dark; it lacks judgment. Everything around me is neutral. Before I know it, I'm almost back home. Things now seem clearer, simpler. All it takes sometimes is a walk, with a breeze, the chill of night, stars in the sky, and stones under your feet.

Prevail to being yourself:

I can tell my presence brings about a feeling of awkwardness in you. My questions pry, opening you to an uncomfortable vulnerability not used to. As if someone who cares puts you in a place of unfamiliarity. Feeling as though you can't be yourself, so it seems. After all, being yourself is something you have avoided for quite some time. This alter ego you have made into your permanent self. Hiding who you really are behind it. Never seeming to have the courage to reveal it. Maybe in time, your synthetic sense of authenticity will be peeled away, giving way to your true identity. It's you, and only you, who can find the salvation of peace, in knowing that you can finally live within, and outside of your true self.